Our Village Church

St Agnes - Cornwall

Clive Benney & Tony Mansell

Wheal Hawke Publications

First Published August 2007 by
Wheal Hawke Publications:

14 Trevaunance Road
St Agnes
Cornwall
TR5 0SE

Cover design by Daniel Benney
www.danielbenney.co.uk

Cover picture is a painting of the Church by Carol Buscombe

ISBN 0-9550510-2-9

Printed by R. Booth Ltd
Antron Hill
Mabe
Penryn
Cornwall
TR10 9HH

Contents

Foreword

As the tenth Vicar of St Agnes Church I need no convincing that the well arranged pile of stone and slate that dominates the centre of our village is a special place. It is special because it is beautiful and well cared for but more than this, as this little book will reveal, it is special as a place where people have encountered God for well over 600 years. Today if you were to go there and take a look you would find many comments in the visitors book speaking of the peace and tranquility that can be had by simply sitting in the building and absorbing some of the atmosphere of prayer - that which has been strangely created by all those who have offered their thoughts to God there through the centuries.

It will always be true to say that Church in its greatest sense is a word that describes a gathered community of people rather than a building but it is perhaps equally true that the quality of the gathering depends upon the sense of sacred space they are able to create. Through the centuries the people of St Agnes have created the space, which is the Church today. These were real people and thus it is no surprise that the Church has attached to it a good many real life stories, stories that link the history of the building and its furnishings to the history of village life and the lives of its residents. You will find a good few stories recorded here, which, perhaps in both senses of the word, form part of the history of St Agnes Church.

Building on the excellent work of Maurice and Alice Bizley, Clive Benney and Tony Mansell have done much in researching further the recorded and oral history of the Church. We are indebted to them for their labours for which they will receive no financial reward - all funds received from this exercise will be put to the task of maintaining the aforementioned special place for the generations that are yet to come.

I hope that part of the pleasure you derive from reading on is the knowledge that you have now contributed to that task.

Alan G Bashforth
St Agnes Vicarage
July 2007

Church Life

Before William the Conqueror landed at Hastings a large Celtic monastery centred on the Parish of Perranzabuloe and with the ancient title of Pieranus in Cornugallia, held the manor of Lampiran - now Perranzabuloe but from 1046 the Sees of Crediton and Cornwall were united at Exeter and the bishopric of Cornwall was suspended. Maurice Bizley says in his book Friendly Retreat that the Saxons were encroaching on the manor even before the Norman, Robert of Mortain, took possession in 1076.

The manor passed to Robert's son and then to the King before it was restored to Church control – to the Cathedral Church in Exeter. It would take 800 years before it was restored to Cornish hands, when Bishop Benson was consecrated Bishop of Truro.

The historian, Charles Henderson, wrote, *"...in the early 12th century the Cathedral Treasury (of Exeter) contained the charter of Bishop Robert (1138-61) confirming St Peranus to the Dean and Chapter. From that time onwards this body owned the Church lands of Lamberran and the advowson of the Church, no longer collegiate, but now a Rectory with St Agnes as a daughter Church."*

In 1925 the Vicar, William H Browne, quoted the historian, Hals, when he wrote, *"At the time of the Conqueror's tax there was no such parish or district of St Agnes; but the same passed in rates under the jurisdiction of the Earl of Cornwall's Manor, now Duchy, of Tywarnhaile; together with Perransand...*

The present Church of St Agnes was of old only a small free Chapel dedicated to her, without endowment, till the same was augmented and rebuilt, of three roofs, as it now stands, by charitable collections and the proper charge and cost of the inhabitants thereof, in 1484, consecrated and dedicated to the honour of Almighty God, in the name of St Agnes, as a daughter church to Perransand, by Dr Peter Courtnay, then Bishop of Oxon.

The Parish Feast is holden on the Sunday following St Agnes day." (Church Magazine)

Writing in the third St Agnes Museum Trust Journal, Ann Preston-Jones states that the earliest reference to the parish is in 1327 - when it was called Parochia Sancte Agnetis.

The Church is dedicated to St Agnes and the belief is that she was a Roman girl, only thirteen years old, when she suffered martyrdom for her faith. Agnes had made a promise to God never to stain her purity. Her love for the Lord was very great and she hated sin even more than death. Since she was very beautiful, many young men wished to marry her but she would always say, *"Jesus Christ is my only Spouse".*

Procop, the Governor's son, became very angry when she refused him. He had tried to win her for his wife with rich gifts and promises but the beautiful young girl kept saying, *"I am already promised to the Lord of the Universe. He is more splendid than the sun and the stars, and He has said He will never leave me!"* In great anger Procop accused her of being a Christian and brought her to his father, the Governor. He asked her to recant her decision and she was told to, *"Remember, you are but a child".*

She replied, *"I may be a child but faith dwells not in years but in the heart".*

The Governor promised Agnes wonderful gifts if she would only deny God, but she refused. He tried to change her mind by putting her in chains but her lovely face shone with joy. Next he sent her naked to a place of sin but an Angel protected her. At last she was condemned to be burnt. Even the pagans cried to see such a young and beautiful girl going to her death. But Agnes was as happy as a bride on her wedding day. She paid no attention to those who begged her to save herself. *"I would offend my Spouse,"* she said, *"if I were to try to please you. He chose me first and He shall have me!"* As the flames rose around her she prayed, *"I bless Thee O Father of my Lord Jesus Christ".* But the flames went out and all attempts to re-light the fire were unsuccessful. Agnes prayed and bowed her head for the death-stroke of the sword. She was martyred in the year 304 AD.

St Agnes is the patron saint of young girls and it is said that in rural areas these girls practised all sorts of quaint country magic on St Agnes Eve to discover who their future husbands would be.

Many refer to our village of St Agnes as St Anns and the Revd S Baring-Gould in A Book of the West suggests that it takes its name from Ann, the mother of the gods amongst the Irish Celts but this may be based on the fact that there are many Cornish places named after Irish saints. Ann Preston-Jones states that, *"Anne is a Hebrew name and a common colloquial version of St Agnes"*.

Dr T F G Dexter in Cornwall, the Land of the Gods, traces the name *"St Ann's"* back to *"San Tan. – Ancient Fire or Holy Fire,"* which places the name in the days of pagan Fire Worship. He adds, *"To subscribe to this proposition there is no need to doubt the existence of St Agnes; all that is needed is to doubt her connection with the parish"*.

Ann Preston-Jones also suggests the possibility that the name may have been derived from the local language. *"The Cornish word 'stenes' bears a superficial resemblence to the name 'St Agnes' and is even closer to the colloquial name St Annis. Stenes is an adjectival form of the word stean, 'tin', plus the suffix -es, 'place of.' 'Place of tin' would certainly be a fitting name for the area."* If you would like to pursue this debate then a fuller version can be found in the 3rd Journal of the St Agnes Museum Trust.

Of course, none of this may be true and it could be that it is simply the Cornish practice of abbreviating names – the *"g"* in Agnes is dropped and we have St Anns.

The local historian, Thomas Tonkin of Trevaunance, wrote, *"But notwithstanding this grant* (the 1482 grant from the Bishop of Exeter to build what we refer to as the second Church), *the said Chapel or Church (for so it is called in an old parchment in my custody, bearing the date 4th July 1396, 86 years before the building of this present church, Edmund Stafford being then Lord Bishop of Exeter) had a parish and parishioners distinct from other parishes…By which it appears that it was only on the more solemn days, such as on the Feast of St Piran etc that the inhabitants of the Parish of St Agnes were obliged to repair to the Mother Church, whatever the Parishioners of St Piran may allege to the contrary."*

From long before the Reformation and up until 1846 St Agnes, despite having the largest population in the Parish of Perranzabuloe, was just a chapelry to the main church at Perranporth. In 1374, the feud between St Agnes and Perran came to a head and Bishop Brantyngham of Exeter placed St Agnes under an Interdict because it refused to obey certain regulations he had made to adjust its relations with the Parish Church of Perran. The main cause of dissatisfaction was that most of the people of the Parish lived in the St Agnes portion but there was no right of burial, except at the Perran Churchyard.

In one of his papers local historian John King wrote, *"In the early days the people of St Agnes had no right of sepulture and were unable to receive the Sacraments, only by attending the mother church at St Piranus in Zabulo. The distance between the two places was great, the roads badly kept, often corpses of the dead fell from the bier, people died without receiving the Sacraments and children were un-baptised, so in 1482 a petition was presented to the Bishop of Exeter and the right to consecrate a Chapel of St Agnes with a cemetery was granted; it was also decreed that the Sacraments should be performed by a resident chaplain."*

The full text of the Bishop's decision is given in Friendly Retreat. It contains many duties and privileges including, in John King's words, *"Prior to this time it was customary for the parishioners of Perran to carry the relics of St Piran on the capsule containing them, to the daughter Church at St Agnes, in Rogation week; they were, it is said, honourably received by the inhabitants in processional array and to be exposed for their veneration. In return, on the Feast of St Piran, the Wardens of St Agnes offered half a pound of wax to the image of St Piran in the Parish Church."*

Donald Blight returned home from Active Service in 1947 and became a Server. He recalled the Rogationtide Processions where the congregation paraded the streets of St Agnes with stops at Pelham Gripe's Field near Castle House, Wheal Friendly and the Vicarage Lawn.

Looking at a wider history perspective it was in 1497 that the people of Cornwall twice took up arms against their king – Henry VII. Michael Joseph, (An Gof) a blacksmith from St Keverne and Thomas Flamanck, a lawyer from Bodmin, led the rebellion in protest at the heavy taxation voted by Parliament for the King's Scottish war. It culminated in a battle at Blackheath when many were killed and the leaders brutally executed.

Later in the year there was a second rebellion but this was much more than a protest. It was in support of Perkin Warbeck who claimed to be Richard, Duke of York, the rightful king of England, but as it spread across the South-West the Pretender chose to desert his cause and leave his supporters to their fate.

St Agnes, in common with almost every parish of Cornwall, was involved in this rebellion and was heavily punished for its participation. Someone from each parish was appointed to collect fines for this," *Contempt against the said King made and committed*". In his book, Tudor Cornwall, A L Rowse states, "*Master Alexander Penhill, rector of Illogan, was responsible for several parishes: Illogan 5 marks, Redruth £4, Camborne £4,...St Agnes 5 marks...*" Richard David of St Agnes was named as one of the sureties for the inhabitants of this parish. (Portrait of a Village Church)

Rowse concludes his story of the episode by saying, "*The effect of the Risings, and perhaps even more of their punishment with such economic severity at a time when currency was scarce, must have been heavy upon Cornish Society...*"

The people of Cornwall were beginning to acquire a reputation for being of a rebellious nature and many English commentators talked of the Cornish in very derogatory terms.

Perhaps we need to remind ourselves that at the time the Church of 1484 was being built and up until the Reformation, this was a Roman Catholic nation with deference to the Pope. Henry VIII's actions caused a split from the Church of Rome and placed him at the head of the English Church. To what extent the Reformation affected St Agnes we are not sure but it is possible that for the ordinary worshipper in Cornwall there was little immediate change.

During the reigns of Edward VI Catholicism was heavily suppressed and The Act of Uniformity brought to a head the unrest which had existed since the beginning of the Reformation. This Act prohibited the use of the Roman Catholic Mass and enforced the use of the first English Prayer Book. Very few Cornish people could read or understand Latin but the Mass was familiar to them and they saw no reason to change. Led by a number of local gentry the people of Cornwall rebelled against this imposition.

The Wynslades (various spellings) of Tregarrick, Pelynt, took an active part in the uprising against their King and in defence of the existing order of service. They also owned the Manor of Mithian so there can be little doubt that men from St Agnes were involved. The revolt became known as the Prayer Book Rebellion or, in some circles, the Cornish Commotion.

John Wynslade was one of the leaders and after a series of battles and a great deal of bloody retribution he was found guilty of treason and hanged, drawn and quartered at Tyburn in 1550.

His son, William, had lived at Mithian Manor and was also involved in the uprising but he managed to avoid execution. In A History of Cornwall, F E Halliday says that William Winslade was, "*... an impoverished Catholic exile, who led a walking life with his harp to gentlemen's houses, wherethrough, and by his other qualities, he was entitled Sir Tristram; ...*"

Because of their involvement Henry VI confiscated the manor house and lands at Mithian and gave them to the Mohun family.

Historians disagree about why the new Prayer book was not translated into Cornish but most accept that the failure to do so was the reason that English became the main language in the Duchy.

In his book West Britons, Mark Stoyle states, "*During the summer of 1549 the rebels were cut to ribbons by government forces. For those who sought to resist assimilation, this defeat had calamitous implications. Now there could be no hope of returning to the old, accommodating Catholic faith, no hope of resisting the English Liturgy. By forcing Protestantism on the Cornish, it seemed, the government would force Englishness upon them too.*"

This was a major conflict and it is ironic that we celebrate in song a threatened rebellion in defence of Bishop Jonathan Trelawney but ignore this actual uprising that changed Cornish history and cost so many lives.

At this time the religious leaning of the country was very fluid as it tilted back towards Catholic Mary and then to Elizabeth who re-introduced Protestantism. Both sides committed atrocities in the name of religion and we are left to wonder how this affected the people of St Agnes as they worshipped in their Parish Church.

The Dean and Chapter of Exeter visited St Agnes in November 1608 and this brought trouble for a few as can be seen from an article by historian Charles Henderson in The West Briton of the 19th July 1928. *"At St Agnes the local gentry were in trouble. Simon George, gentlemen, and Richard Cleder were presented 'for brawling and scolding in Church;' Peter Beacham, gentleman, 'for using unseemly speeches and railing words in the Church'. Salathiel George and Edward George, gentlemen, for the like; and Margaret, wife of John Paull, 'for scolding in the churchyard' with Katherine, wife of Richard Danyell. They were all excommunicated, paid their fines, and received absolution. Last of all, Margaret Plemyn, alias Chinoweth, executrix of John Plemyn, late Vicar of Perran, was excommunicated for allowing the 'House of the Curate' at St Agnes to be much decayed and refusing to restore it."*

The book Friendly Retreat provides information on a few other misdemeanours around this time: *"Roger Trevells excommunicated for not receiving the Communion. Ric. Carrowe excommuni-cated for the like. Geo Martin, ditto, nor any of his household. Parkyn Cooke was presented for absenting himself from Church. Tho. Rowe was excommunicated for 'bowling on the Saboth daie at Lente Time' and Jo Crocker, Wm Rodgers, Jo Gathcomb and Tho. Allinge were presented for unrever-ently behaving themselves in the Church at the time of Divine Service and for 'hunting on the Saboth daie'."*

The extent to which the Duchy was involved in the English Civil War is not widely appreciated. Many skirmishes and battles took place on Cornish soil and its people were involved in the fighting across the South-West. Cornwall stood foursquare for the King although this was by no means a certainty at the commencement of hostilities. Even now there are doubts whether this was due to the suggested *"love and affection for our King"* or because of fear that a Parliamentarian victory would not suit Cornwall.

It is easy to see the Civil War as yet another religious conflict and some historians believe this to be the case. Since Henry the VIII the country had followed successive monarchs as they championed the cause of either Catholicism or Protestantism. Then along came Charles, a Danish Scot, who had married a Catholic and who did not hide the fact that he was receptive to the Church returning to a traditional form of ritual and idolatry. Catholicism by the back door? Maybe! The Puritan members of Parliament thought so and they resolved to oppose him.

The Cornish Prayer Book Rebellion of 1549 evidences that there had been a reluctance to forsake Catholicism, Protestantism had been adopted but only after a considerable struggle. This conservative attitude makes it unlikely that the new Puritan teaching would have penetrated the Cornish speaking areas of the Duchy. Any movement in religious leanings was almost certainly to be back towards the high church rather than to the new simpler form. But while the Catholic issue is often quoted as the catalyst for the conflict, the combatants were not drawn up along these clear religious lines; many Catholics opposed the King and some Puritans could not bring themselves to draw swords against him. Religious divisions certainly played their part but recent commentators see the problem as more complex than suggested by this simplistic explanation.

This was a time of increasing enlightenment; Parliament's role of acquiescence to the King was approaching its end and for many the idea that God appointed the King with a divine right to rule was an anathema. Before long the Levellers and Diggers would find their voice and for them even the comparative equality under Cromwell was not sufficient.

But if people could go along with the religious shift and even accept that the King was supreme in all things, then there was a third factor which caused considerable unrest - the affect of his actions on their pocket. The King's failed foreign policy and his ostentatiousness and extravagance contributed to the high level of taxation in the country and many were thrown into prison for refusing to pay.

In the past Cornwall had rebelled against high taxation and now Charles had imprisoned some of its notables for withholding payment. Taxation in respect of the wars in Scotland must have been particularly galling considering the Duchy's remoteness from that country. Ship Money was more understandable and relevant to the area and coastal protection from France and Spain and even the Barbary Pirates was necessary but, even so, the high level of taxation made life difficult for this relatively poor area.

But there was one further issue which is sufficiently compelling to explain the Cornish support for the monarchy.

In many areas the Duchy was still seen as a foreign country - certainly amongst the men of the Parliamentarian Army. Perhaps its remoteness from London; the fact that many of its people spoke a different language; and certainly its history contributed to that view. It was clear that the new order being pioneered by Parliament was a threat to the relative autonomy that Cornwall enjoyed and the destruction of The Duchy Palace at Lostwithiel was seen by many as a deliberate move to obliterate a semblance of independence. The potential loss of its Stannary Laws and the homogeneous nature of their central policies would make it just like any other county. To the people of Cornwall that was not acceptable.

Whether out of loyalty or self-interest the people of Cornwall defended the King's cause with many lost in defence of its land and on *"foreign"* soil. No doubt St Agnes sent its share of combatants and certainly received the famous letter of thanks from Charles I – copies of which are still displayed in many Cornish churches. Unfortunately the one at St Agnes has disappeared – perhaps during the rebuilding process or at the hand of some over-zealous official during Cromwell's *"reign"*. Another possibility is that it was lodged with the parent Church at Perranzabuloe.

The loyalty of the people of St Agnes is reflected in the treatment meted out to Michael Stuckey, Minister of St Agnes and Perranzabuloe, by the Commonwealth Parliament. Dr Walker, in his book Sufferings of the Clergy, published in 1714, does not mention Stuckey by name because this information arrived too late for insertion in his work.

"April 13, 1715. Tho. Tonkin, Esq. of St Agnes in the County of Cornwall gave me an account that Mr Michael Stuckey, formerly minister of St Agnes aforesaid and of Perran in Sabulo in the said County was in time of the Rebellion against King Charles deprived of both his livings for his loyalty to the King and was not only denied the 5th part of his said livings, but was also taxed for the 5th and 20th parts of his Temporal Estate. For which last particular he also showed me an Instrument in writing under the hand of the Secretary to the Committee of Parliament in Cornwall dated in June 1646 summoning not only Mr Stuckey but Mr Tho. Tonkin of St Agnes, grandfather to the aforesaid Tho. Tonkin Esq. to come in and pay what they were assessed on the aforementioned account."

In 1660 the restoration of the monarchy was celebrated and the Coat of Arms of Charles II displayed in the Church commemorates this.

The reference to language is interesting as well as confusing. There is little doubt that the advancement of English as the main spoken language took place progressively from the east to the west of Cornwall and over a great number of years. In West Britons, Mark Stoyle suggests that the whole process could have been spread over 500 years and from his diagrams it is clear that the Cornish language was still quite common in St Agnes in the 1600s – at the time of the Civil War.

James Vowler is described as a *"zealous evangelical priest"*. He was in charge at St Agnes in the 1750s when John Wesley visited the Church and described how he had heard him preach *"two such thundering sermons"*.

It is well recorded that John Wesley visited St Agnes on many occasions and attended services at the Church where he was, *"Generally well received"*. His journal for the 18th September 1762 states, *"I preached once more in the street at Redruth and in St Agnes in the evening. I preached again at eight in the morning and afterwards heard an excellent sermon at the Church, preached by the Rector, Mr Walker, elder brother to the late Mr Walker of Truro. He likewise gave notice of his design to preach in the afternoon a funeral service for Mr Phelps, his late curate, a man eminently humble, serious and zealous for God. He was snatched away by a fever three weeks since, as was his predecessor, Mr Vowler, three or four years before…"*

The Revd Thomas Wills was Curate at Perranzabuloe in 1762 with special responsibility for St Agnes. Maurice Bizley says, *"He attended shipwrecks and had a great restraining influence on the plundering tendencies of the populace of those days"*.

On the 2nd of February 1778 the Sherborne Mercury included an advertisement in its *"Situation Vacant"* column. *"St Agnes: Wanted A Resident Curate to serve the Parish. The salary between £40 and £50 a year and the tythes of Goose, Pig and Honey. If the gentleman will take the trouble of collecting the tythes and offerings he shall have 10 guineas more yearly. Application to be made to the Revd Mr Walker at Lanlivery."*

This item from the Church Magazine seeks to identify the start of Sunday schools. *"Mining was flourishing – the first steam engine for pumping was installed in the Parish, a Boulton and Watt 40 at Seal Hole – the American colonists were fighting for independence...the Industrial Revolution was attracting workers to the factories in the towns and the restraints of village life were gone. In Gloucester Robert Raikes was concerned with the way the children ran wild on Sundays – swearing, rough and ragged. The rest of the week they worked long hours. So he hired teachers and started Sunday schools for them which improved their behaviour so much that he commended the idea in his weekly newspaper, The Gloucester Journal. This was taken up by others and by 1785 there were many more Sunday schools in the country."*

On the 15th of November 1786 a letter appeared in the Sherborne Mercury - from The Curate, Cornwall. It praised, *"An institution so essential to the interest of religion and morals as Sunday schools,"* and told of his success in one of the most considerable Mining Parishes in the county. It went on to say, *"Owing to insufficiency of funds the number of our objects at this time is four hundred and fifty who were in a state of rudeness and ignorance, undisciplined and uninformed. But the reformation and improvement in four months is really astonishing."*

Writing in the Church Magazine in March 1986, W H Morrison suggests that although the letter is only signed *"The Curate,"* it must have been sent by the Revd William Harpur of St Agnes as the account books of Trevaunance Mine shows an annual payment to the Revd Wm Harpur for the Sunday school.

On the 3rd of August 1789 the Sherborne Mercury announced that the Revd Wm Harpur, Curate of St Agnes, had been killed when he was thrown from a one-horse chaise. It said, *"With a few frailties (and who is there without them?) he possessed many excellent qualities and his exertions to promote Sunday school in the parish will perpetuate his generosity and goodness of heart to future generations"*.

"So," says Bill Morrison, *"St Agnes had the first reported Sunday school in Cornwall - in July 1786"*.

For his show of courage the Reverend W H Snowe deserves a mention in our history. He was the curate in the 1830s, at the time of the cholera outbreak at Mount Hawke. With obvious admiration for his courage Maurice Bizley wrote, *"During the whole time that the scourge raged, the Revd Snowe visited and ministered to the stricken people, quite ignoring the great danger in which he placed himself"*.

Edward Montague Hamilton was curate in the 1830s and until the first Vicar was appointed. He became the first Vicar at Mount Hawke, in 1847.

Writing in the St Agnes Museum Trust Journal, Betty Tredinnick describes village life up to about 1840. *"As the church was the legal entity in the parish and as attendance was compulsory four times a year, the position of parson was important and powerful. In the early part of the 19th century the patrons of the living of Perranzabuloe and St Agnes were the Buller family of Crediton; they used to send a parson here with a salary of £100 a year. On top of this considerable salary the parson could claim a tithe (tenth) of everything grown in the parish. This was often paid in kind with every tenth sheaf having to be set aside for him at harvest and a tenth part of any honey taken from a stock of bees brought to the Vicarage. This was always the white comb, the best part!*

The church was also responsible for training parish apprentices; children who had become chargeable to the parish because their parents were either dead or destitute.

At the other end of life, when people became incapable of work or providing for themselves, the parish was also responsible for them. They were sent to Alms Houses which were situated opposite the stables used by a Mr Hooper – now Presingoll Barns."

The St Agnes Parish Council Resolution Book reflects the harsh times of the 1840s with entries like, *"Money paid out to… for clothing her family"* and, *"Money paid out for passage to South Australia".* It resolved that, *"The Church Wardens and Overseers shall raise the sum of £60 as a fund for defraying the expenses of the emigration of poor persons having settlements in this parish and being allowed to emigrate".* Not for nothing was the period referred to as the, *"hungry forties".* (Jericho to Cligga)

In 1846 it was a case of *"all change"* as St Agnes was separated from Perranzabuloe and became an independent ecclesiastical Parish. Mithian and Mount Hawke Parishes were created at the same time. The Revd Alexander Allen Vawdrey was appointed the first Vicar of St Agnes on the 1st of May and it was under his leadership that the new Church was built.

A religious census of the 31st March 1851 records a Tithe of £250 *"...tenth of annual produce of agriculture etc payable for support of priesthood, religious establishments, etc now converted into rent charge".* It shows that the Church had 600 free sittings and the average attendance was 100 in the morning and 400 in the afternoon.

An article in the West Briton of the 6th June 1851 bemoans some 19th century vandalism. *"Some miscreants have for some months past infested the neighbourhood of St Agnes and committed a number of petty depredations and much wanton mischief.*

In April last much annoyance was occasioned to the Wesleyan Missionary deputation who had hired a carriage at Truro to take them to St Agnes to hold a meeting there with the intention of returning to Truro the same night but during the missionary service someone carried off the pole of the carriage, in consequence of which they were detained overnight. Some days after the pole was found in the Parish Church.

The day previously to the one on which the new Church was consecrated someone had the hardihood to enter the vestry and carry off the gown and surplice belonging to the Vicar, thereby necessitating the Reverend Gentleman to meet the Bishop the next day in borrowed canonicals. Both articles however have since been found and restored to their owner.

About a week ago a valuable horse belonging to the Wesleyan Minister of St Agnes was greatly disfigured by having its tail and mane sheared and no later than Monday night last a horse belonging to Mr John James, van proprietor, was treated in a similar manner."

1875 - The Revd Alexander Allen Vawdrey died and was buried in the old burial ground.

1875 - The Revd Edward Lister Salisbury was appointed Vicar of St Agnes.

Preston Tregellas caused a furore in 1883 and was required to apologise to the Church; his letters are lodged at the County Records Office. It seems however that they were not considered sufficient and he was forced to print and display this notice in St Agnes.

"I Preston Vincent Tregellas hereby humbly Apologise to the Church, Church Wardens and Congregation of St Agnes Parish Church, for my misbehaviour in that Church on Sunday the 8th January last in disturbing them during Divine Service by distributing a Tract issued by the Liberation Society. I pledge myself not to repeat the offence and undertake to immediately pay all the costs of any

incident to the prosecution brought against me in respect of such offence and I consent that this Apology be printed for distribution in St Agnes. Signed Preston V Tregellas 22nd February 1883."

The tract in question began, *"Reader! Do you not think it is high time the Government left off making laws for the support of religion and let the people look after their own spiritual interests: in other words that the Church must be separated from the State?"* We are left to wonder whether it was the occasion or the message which caused the greater offence but it does show the considerable influence that the Church had on people's lives and actions at that time.

1886 - The Revd Edward Lister Salisbury resigned his position of Vicar of St Agnes.

1887 – The Revd Alfred Rudall was appointed Vicar of St Agnes.

Towards the end of the 19th century Cornwall's only Cathedral was built. An article on its website states, "Truro was not the only candidate for the siting of the Cathedral. Bodmin had been the medieval ecclesiastical centre of Cornwall, while the original Cornish See of St Germans also put forward a claim. The Vicar of St Columb also offered his Church! The merits of each place were much discussed

The Revd Alfred Rudall

and argued over. Eventually a Bill establishing the Diocese of Truro was finally passed by Parliament, on the 11th August 1876. The site chosen in Truro was where the Parish Church of St Mary's stood. To build a Cathedral on this site meant that a number of properties on the northern side of the proposed development had to be bought and demolished. This was duly completed by 1880."

"A visitor to St Agnes" wrote the following item to the West Briton in September 1891.
"Sir – Can anything be done to put a stop to the disgraceful conduct of many so-called 'worshippers' in the church at St Agnes? Visitors are much annoyed and greatly astonished at the manners of the young men, boys and girls, who come to church there, but who frequently laugh and talk the whole time.

There are some who sit all through the service, too lazy to stand during the singing of Psalms and hymns, and, of course, who never dream of kneeling during the prayers (some, of course, may be invalids or cripples, but those I refer to appear strong and well). The boys naturally follow the young men's example, and rows of children sit together without any grown-up person to look after them; so the evil grows.

The visitors note these things with astonishment, and St Agnes people must surely know that such want of reverence is a disgrace and a blot on their growing town and fine church. What are the churchwardens or sidesmen that they allow such things to continue? Perhaps sitting high up in the church they are not aware of what is going on near the doors. One remedy I would suggest is that they, or someone in authority, should sit at the bottom of the church near the doors and font, where they can see for themselves what goes on, and keep some sort of order. It will be a pity to drive visitors away, and it is certainly already making a difference, as some are finding the service entirely spoilt to them, and do not care to go to witness what is a most distressing scene."

As the century drew to a close the talk was of war - in Africa against the Boers. Many local men took up arms to fight for the Empire but it was a conflict which was to eventually prick this nation's conscience.

In 1902 a faculty was issued concerning correspondence and *"Statement of Facts,"* relating to a Case brought by the Vicar and Church Wardens of St Agnes and the St Agnes Burial Board regarding items of Church property which were taken from the Church grounds and used in the burial ground.

Under the heading of *"Old v New tunes"* the Royal Cornwall Gazette of the 26th of March 1903 included an item which could be thrown up by every generation. We are not sure that it was related specifically to church music but it is interesting. *"The old tunes which were common 30, 50 or even 100 years ago are being revived. The older folk hold that there is but little music in many of the metrical tunes of today and they are not far wrong, but although the repetition in the old style at times are rather comical, yet in many of them there is undoubtedly something which carries one away with the music and which something is absent from the metrical tunes of today."*

On the 13th of August 1903 the Royal Cornwall Gazette records that, *"The choir of the Parish Church had their annual outing on Thursday to Carbis Bay where a pleasant time was spent".*

This newspaper report in August 1904 is of interest both from a Church and secular point of view. *"The choir of the Parish Church visited Penzance on Thursday in connection with their annual outing. The party drove to Redruth and took the train there for the westernmost borough as by this means they secured a later train back. It seems a pity that the GWR authorities do not give us later trains (to and from) than we now have.*

That will probably come when the connection with Newquay is an accomplished fact."

The Church Choir outside the Vicarage circa 1905

The Royal Cornwall Gazette of the 3rd of August 1905 reported, *"On Friday, teachers and scholars of St Agnes Church held their annual tea-treat. For several years rain had spoilt the effort but beautifully fine weather contributed to a successful tea which was held in Castle House grounds."*

Sunday school teachers circa 1905

At a Vestry meeting on the 30th of April 1908 Messrs T Martin and J Eudey were re-elected as Church Wardens and T Rogers, W Vanstone, W Johns and C Harper as Sidesmen.

Mr Eudey asked what steps had been or were about to be taken regarding the covered way from the vestry to the Church. Mr Rogers thought that the work ought to be done before the summer visitors arrived and that, *"The money could easily be got".*

Mr Rogers then asked whether the Vicar would consent to the doors of the Church being unlocked during the summer months. The extended exchange between the two men does not lose its edge even after so many years have passed but despite all efforts the Vicar held firm. It seems that many years previous the Church doors were not locked but owing to children going in and dressing up in cassocks and surplices and performing mock marriages the decision to lock them was made. Mr Rogers considered that current day children were better behaved. *"I hope so,"* countered the Vicar but the doors remained locked.

Thanks were passed to the executors of the late Mr Carne for the gift of an oak chest for the safe keeping of the altar frontals. It was the first meeting to be held in the new vestry built by the late Mr William Naylor Carne (dedicated after his death) in memory of his son, Alfred Wilmot Carne, who had died in South Africa in 1897. (RCG 30/4/1908)

On the 27th of February 1908 the Royal Cornwall Gazette included a lengthy item about an event of some note. *"The Oddfellows Hall was packed on Friday evening to witness a performance of Dick Whittington and his Cat by young people connected with the Parish Church. The performance was a capital one and was thoroughly enjoyed by those present. Those taking part were: Mr Pelham Gripe (Dick Whittington), Mr John Rowles (The cat), Mrs C Harris (Alderman Fitzwarren), Miss Olive Richards (Jenny, the Alderman's daughter), Mr Jack Langdon (Jenny's brother), Miss Rudall (the Alderman's cook), Miss Laura Richards (housemaid), Mr Charles Harper (King of Barbary), Miss K Nile (Queen of Barbary), Miss L Nile (Princess), Miss Ada Roberts (German singer), Mr T Rogers (Capt Sailaway), Mr Parker (Captain's mate), Mr W Bennetts (Simon), Mr Roland Roberts (Jester), Misses Henwood, Richards, Sanders, Lockett, Osborne and Chapman (fairies), Master Harris, C Richards, Roberts and E Richards (black attendants), Masters W Roberts, C Ireland, H Osborne, W Welsh, H Stribley and N Benney (Aldermen). Mr Delbrdge was at the piano and the Revd J Rowan and Mr L Bryant were the stage managers.*

The proceeds were in aid of the Boys Brigade. As a large number were unable to witness the performance on Friday the entertainment was repeated on Saturday."

Most churches and chapels held an annual outing for their choirs and in July 1908 it was reported that the Church Choir had a *"Pleasant day at Fowey".*

Two snippets from the Royal Cornwall Gazette of the 25th of February 1909:

"Mrs Naylor Carne has given a very valuable set of altar clothes to the Parish Church."
"In aid of the funds of the Church Football Club, a social was held on Friday evening."

Hospital Sunday was held on the 8th August 1909 and the Royal Cornwall Gazette reported, *"The parade was headed by the band under John Paull and was followed by, members of the Philanthropic Society, Oddfellows and Rechabite Lodges paraded the streets and attended a service at the Parish Church conducted by the Revd A Rudall. The choir under Miss Rudall rendered the anthem 'Clap your hands,' the solo being taken by Mr M P Radcliffe. The band gave a concert in the evening and was heartily thanked for their gratuitous services on the motion of the Revd C Rickard and Dr Whitworth. The amount secured was .... This will be divided between the Royal Cornwall Infirmary, Redruth Hospital and the District Nursing Association."*

On the 30th of December 1909 the Royal Cornwall Gazette reported on a recent bazaar. It had been opened by Mrs Rawson of Heamoor who was supported by Mrs Rudall, the Revds A Rudall and S J

Richards, Mrs J Eudey and Dr Lindsay. The Vicar explained that the funds raised would be used to complete the covered way from the Church to the new vestry and for lighting and heating the Church.

Stallholders included: Mesdames Rudall, Whitworth, Chapman, Delbridge and Gripe (Fancy goods), Misses Richards, Lockett, Comer, Thomas and Rowles (Toys), Misses A J & B Hicks (China), Mesdames Jones, Cowling, Martin, Misses Sloggett, Harris and Gordon (Refreshments). Messrs T Rogers, Johns, Harper, Whitworth, Rowles and Radcliffe (Gent's stall).

In August 1910 an alfresco dance was held on the croquet lawn of Castle House. The funds were in aid of the Church Sunday school. (RCG 18/8/1910)

The ladies preparing the food for the 1910 tea-treat

The Coronation of King George V took place on the 22nd June 1911. The morning was marred by continuous rain but by the afternoon the weather had improved. The village was well decorated and the festivities commenced with a service in the Parish Church. The afternoon events were held in a field at Penwinnick and St Agnes Town Band accompanied the singing. (St Agnes and its Band)

Tea-treats have largely been confined to history and it may be that many today will not appreciate their significance to the church and the community in general. Everything seemed to stop for the occasion and in some of the smaller communities it was the biggest event on the calendar. The majority of people attending were local but visitors were also made welcome. The venue may have been someone's large garden or a suitable field. The grass would have been cut, decorations erected and a number of tables placed in position to act as stalls or for the preparation of food.

The event commenced with a procession led by the banner carriers. Each chapel or church had its own banner and it was proudly carried at the front of the procession as a testament to the members' faith. Immediately behind them would be the band followed by the children and the adults. The route often seemed endless but eventually the procession returned to the tea-treat field and the band took its place in readiness for the official opening.

A local dignitary usually opened the day and the band then started its afternoon programme. To this background music various competitions and sports took place for the children and often for the grown-ups as well.

At some appropriate point the children were given their tea-treat bun - a huge saffron bun which was certainly larger than the ones in the shops today. Whatever else people remember about these events these buns are always mentioned. Tea was always a high spot and when the children had finished it was the turn of the band and no matter how hungry (or greedy) they were, it just kept on coming. No committee worth its salt was going to send the band home hungry. (St Agnes and its Band)

On the 3rd August 1911 it was St Agnes Church Sunday school tea-treat. Mr H. Robins was by now conducting the band and the photograph shows them parading through Churchtown. The Royal Cornwall Gazette reported, *"Rain in the evening spoilt the enjoyment somewhat"*.

Members of the Sunday school pause for the photographer in Churchtown in 1911

The Church Sunday school tea-treat in July 1912 was again spoilt by rain. (RCG)

On the 14th of August 1913 the Royal Cornwall Gazette gave notice that a bazaar and garden fete was to be held in Coulterville grounds and that Miss Mabel Williams of Scorrier would perform the opening ceremony. The Church annual outing had taken place on the previous Friday when, *"A large number attended and journeyed by road in Mr James' conveyances through Perranporth to Newquay where a delightful day was spent. The weather was all that could be wished for. Accompanying the trip were Miss Rudall, Mrs Delbridge and the Revd J Thomas."*

A newspaper report in February 1914 states that the St Agnes Church football club was discontinued due to lack of interest amongst players. These were troubled times, of course, and it may have been that thoughts were elsewhere.

In August 1914 this country was at war again but this time on a scale that was sufficient for it to be referred to as the First World War. Many local men volunteered to serve in the defence of their country and a number of those who took up arms did not return. It was given the ironic title of *"The Great War"* but the casualties numbers were devastating and when it finally drew to a close, in 1918, it was thought that it would be a *"War to end all wars"*. It was sadly not the case.

On the 12th of August 1915 the Royal Cornwall Gazette reported on the Church Sunday school tea-treat held in the fields of Castle House. St Agnes Band, under Mr H Robins, entertained and the old game of *"Kissing in the ring"* was revived. It is perhaps surprising that a game with such a purpose had ever died out.

Enjoying the tea in 1915

Servicemen join in the Church tea celebrations in 1916

Sunday school pupils in 1919

In November 1918 the Armistice was signed and the peace was celebrated across the land.

1922 – The Revd Alfred Rudall resigned his position of Vicar of St Agnes at the age of 82. It is interesting to note that following the introduction of an Ecclesiastical Law in the 1970s Vicars were required to retire at the age of 70.

1923 – The Revd William Henry Browne was appointed Vicar of St Agnes.

Rev. W. H. Browne, The Vicar of St. Agnes, 1922-33.

In his Parish historical notes John King writes, *"It was during the incumbency of the Revd William Henry Browne, from 1922 to 1933, that the Church was beautified as it is now. Prior to his coming Church services were conducted strictly to the Book of Common Prayer but he was one of the High Church School and at the very beginning of his ministry changed the form of service. The Sacrament was reserved – incense was used at the Parish Mass and Evensong was preceded by a Processional. The Angelus was rung three times a day…*

Such services were new to St Agnes and the changes were not at first appreciated by all and caused much opposition from Church people and Nonconformist parishioners alike but Father Browne possessed a strong character and carried on regardless, practising his beliefs, in spite of the many difficulties and soon became admired for his courage and much beloved by the inhabitants generally.

In August of each year a Procession of Witness was held through the streets. Three stations were made; at Peterville, the old burial ground and the Vicarage lawn, with addresses by visiting clergy at each station. These processions were well attended, banners were carried and incense was used."

J Eudey and T Rogers were the Church Wardens and Mr Donald Behenna the Organist and Choirmaster in 1924.

The Church Magazine reported, *"The Revd W H R Trewhella, Assistant Priest of St Paul's, Truro, is coming to us at the beginning of March. His record at the Cathedral under Sub Dean Hassard and at St Paul's is such that St Agnes is to be congratulated on his appointment here."*

Shortly after this appointment the Magazine reported the formation of a boys' club. It said, *"Mr Trewhela manages this and anyone wishing to join must speak to him."*

In 1927 Charles Wadge took over from William Rapson as Organist and Choir Master.

In 1927 the annual carnival was organised by the Revd C V Lawson and Mr Leigh Clark on behalf of the Church and, *"Mrs Bailey, Mrs Evans and Mr Parker (London) were the judges. The outstanding feature and first prize winner was the Special Local Improvement Committee.*

A dance was afterwards held in the marquee, music being supplied by an orchestra from Camborne, the pianist being Mr D Powell. Selections were played by St Agnes Town Band during the afternoon and evening." (RCG 24/8/1927)

There were 160 entries for the 1928 carnival when one of the classes was, *"For a boy or girl in fancy dress costing not more than one shilling"*. Miss Hockley of Feock opened the Church Fair and the festivities included the usual sports events. (RCG 22/8/1928)

In 1933 the Church was dealt a terrible blow when the Revd William Henry Browne died. From the written reports it was clear that the community was greatly affected by the loss of their incumbent Priest – a man who had made a considerable impact on the Church of St Agnes. The Church Magazine included the following obituary.

"On the 4th February, in the still hours of the morning, there passed to his rest William Henry Browne, Priest of God and for the last ten years Vicar of this Parish of St Agnes. His death was as sudden as, humanly speaking, it was tragic.

On the previous day he had attended the opening of Bodrean Home for Tramps, near St Erme. He seemed then to be in good health and spirits but the Angel of Death was already abroad in the land and as evening drew on he spread his wings. Early in the morning of Saturday the 4th February, without suffering, the Vicar was borne to the realm of higher service beyond the veil.

Much has been said in the newspapers concerning the life and labours of Father Browne. We have been told that he held successively four livings, one in New Zealand and three in Cornwall. We know that he was a member of nearly every committee in the Diocese of Truro. Above all we know him to have been a most charming personality - a gentleman in the highest sense of the word. All these things are true. Yet for the secret spring which guided his life and conduct we must look still deeper. A man's worth is not to be measured by multitude of possessions, neither is it to be valued by superficial achievement.

The mainspring which directed the life of Fr Browne was his tremendous sense of vocation. He was above all a priest. He was not only the Vicar of St Agnes but he was the Father of his flock. He had received a commission to feed the sheep of Christ and he did all in his power to see that this commission was carried out. Both formally in the administration of the Sacraments and informally in the capacity of adviser his great aim was the maintenance of unity in the family of God. Under the good providence of God it was this trait in his character, this capacity for affection and loving service, which was responsible for the success of his ministry at St Agnes.

In the near future, perhaps, the parishioners of St Agnes will be asked to place in the Church a monument to his memory. Meanwhile it is sufficient to repeat some words which were said at the Sung Mass on the day after his passing. 'Whoever comes into this Church sees Father Browne.' He loved his Church. The interior of the Church as we know it today is largely his creation. He would never tolerate the shoddy and the second rate in the house of God. Services and furniture alike must be worthy of Him to whom they were to be consecrated and he spared no personal expense to ensure that God's earthly temple should be a temple of light and beauty.

Finally, it must be recorded that he was a devoted son of the Church of England. He believed her to be the Catholic Church of the land – that part of the Church which has been appointed by Almighty God to lead Englishmen into the way of salvation. He believed in her orders and her sacraments and he obeyed her canons to the letter. 'The Lord guided the righteous in the right paths and he showed him the Kingdom of Heaven.'

We will not mourn for him. He has passed into a wider sphere of joy and service. It is sufficient that we pray for him as we know that even now he prays for us.
Grant him, O Lord, eternal rest, and let light everlasting shine upon him."

Under the heading of *"St Agnes Memorial to Late Vicar,"* the Royal Cornwall Gazette of the 13th June 1934 stated, *"The erection of a rood beam in St Agnes Parish Church is the suggested form for a memorial to the late Vicar the Revd W H Browne".*

The Church Magazine confirmed this when it reported, *"I am glad to be able to tell you that, after making one or two small alterations, the Advisory Committee on Faculties has approved Mr Read's design for the Rood Beam which we hope to place in the Church in memory of your late Vicar. I am now awaiting the necessary tracing copy of the design which is to be sent to the Chancellor of the Diocese in London and this will probably be received by the time that this magazine is published. The Chancellor will then issue the faculty. When this has been done, the original coloured design will be placed in the Church for everyone to see and we hope then that Father Browne's many friends will show their affection for him by giving as generously as possible to perpetuate his memory and to make still more beautiful the Church he loved so much. But I think it must be clearly understood that the definite order for the Rood cannot be given to the architect until the whole of the necessary sum, £200, has been subscribed."*

It had been Mr Browne's wish to erect a Rood in the Church but his unexpected death had prevented him from doing so.

1933 - On the 5th of April the St Austell Gazette reported, *"The Dean and Chapter of Truro has offered the living of St Agnes to the Revd Charles Geoffrey Roffe-Silvester MA who has accepted it."*

Donald Blight joined the Church Choir in 1936, aged 11. His mother, Daisy Blight (née Rowles), had sung there since the time of the First World War. Charlie Repper was also a member but within a couple of years of joining he was tragically killed in a bicycle accident. Donald also recalls Alwyn Harris, Alfred Crebo, Cecil Langford, George Repper and Mavis Johns. He said, *"On Sundays it was Morning Service, afternoon Sunday school and Evening Service. I used to try and work it that I had tea with someone to avoid having to go all the way home."*

James Henry Stanaway was a full-time Verger and Sexton. Donald Blight said, *"His duties were quite varied and apart from preparing for services and grave-digging there was the grounds to keep in good order and the boiler to clean out and light. It must have been some time in the 1930s when he retired and although there were others who undertook parts of his role, he was the last person to hold it as a full-time position."*

1937 – The Revd Charles Geoffrey Roffe-Silvester resigned his position of Vicar of St Agnes and non-conformist and church people subscribed to a parting gift, probably in recognition of his unifying roll of bringing the churches closer together. He was to be the new Vicar of St Hilary and Canon F R Carr, who presided over the leaving event said that the Parish was losing a loving and faithful priest.

The Vicar said that he had not been in the Parish very long before he realised that there was not, *"That friendly and Christian feeling between what was commonly called church and chapel that there ought to be"*. He had taken on the task to foster such a spirit.

In thanking everyone for the gift he said that it was entirely out of a sense of duty that he was moving to St Hilary. (St Austell Guardian 11/5/1937)

John King describes how the Anglo-Catholic Priest at St Hilary, the Reverend Bernard Walke, fell foul of the authorities and was ordered to remove certain items from his Church. He wrote, *"In 1936 he resigned owing to ill health and the Revd C G Roffe-Silvester was appointed to the living...to be instituted on 28th September 1936"*. However, a restraining order was placed on the Bishop of Truro which stated that no priest could be appointed to St Hilary until a roll of electors was compiled and a number of parishioners chosen to serve on the Parochial Church Council. All this took time but in due course, and for the second time, the Revd C G Roffe-Silvester was appointed to that benefice. John King said, *"This ended a chapter of ecclesiastical history and St Agnes Parish and its Vicar will be coupled with St Hilary in State records"*.

Canon Fred Carr was a Curate at St Agnes and Donald Blight recalls him as likeable and full of fun. He said, *"We used to tease him and call him Fred. Well, you just didn't do that sort of thing in those days. He didn't mind though and used to pretend to chase after us waving his umbrella"*.

1937 - The Revd Guy Humphrey Barnicoat was appointed Vicar of St Agnes. He had previously served at Tywardreath and succeeded the Revd C G Roffe-Silvester who had moved to St Hilary. (RCG 9/6/1937)

Canon Carr and the
Revd G H Barnicoat

Sunday school tea-treats were usually held either in Pelham Gripe's Field or where Penwinnick Parc now stands. These were large events and always started with a procession led by a brass band.

Sunday school outings were something to look forward to with a bus or train trip to a popular beach – often Carbis Bay.

In 1937, after 11 years as organist, Charles Wadge resigned and the Church Magazine recorded its regret at this loss. Mr Arthur George S Blatchford succeeded him.

War came again in September 1939 and many local men were lost in the defence of our nation.

In 1939 the Church Magazine reflected on the world situation. *"What we have dreaded has come to pass and as The Times says, 'Across the world the line between civilisation and the jungle is drawn'. Is it not rather a war between Christianity and the power of evil? There need be no shadow of doubt about the right or justice of England and France going to war, not against the German people, but against injustice, cruelty, greed and a lust for power.*

But we must not fall into the error of Israel of old, who so often left God out of it. War is not of God but He is a God of justice and truth and we should without hesitation pray to him concerning our enemies in the words of the Prayer Book that he may, 'Abate their pride, assuage their malice and confound their devices'.

Many will be leaving this Parish to serve in the forces, as nurses, on the land and in many other ways. We hope to post all their names in the Church porch so that we may pray for them.

Those left at home will find plenty to do looking after their friends and evacuees from vulnerable areas, making garments, bandages etc But one of the most important things that they can do, and should make time to do, is to offer increasing prayer to Almighty God. Those on active and special service will find little opportunity; it is for us to pray for them. In a Church like ours it is not necessary to arrange special services. We have a daily Mass and Morning and Evening Prayer are said daily, when we pray to 'the author of peace and lover of concord'. Let us make the most of these, not merely for our own comfort, but as a very definite piece of National Service."

It goes on to say, *"The social life of the Parish should continue, as more than ever in times of mental stress, we need relaxation. The Church Hall will conform to black-out regulations and at present all entertainments must end by 10.00pm."*

In 1940 the Magazine refers to a difficulty relating to services during the time of war. *"Owing to the extension of summer time it has been found necessary to black-out all the windows of the Church as even the 8.00 o'clock Mass on Sundays would be held in the official hours of darkness. In spite of the great cost, the Parochial Church Council readily agreed to this being done and we must repay them by supporting well the collections for Church expenses.*

The daily Evensong, including Sundays, will continue at 3.00pm as, during the cold, wild, stormy weather which we are bound to have to face, we feel that this hour will be most suitable for the majority.

But there are some who find the dark mornings very difficult for attending Mass. Therefore, during the winter months, the hour of Mass on Friday mornings will vary so that the service is held after black-out is lifted. We ask you therefore to listen carefully on Sundays or to check the time on the Church Services Notice on the board in the Church Porch."

Angela Pakeman recalled her Confirmation when the candidates were checked over by the Nuns of the Epiphany who ensured that they were, *"Decently clad, covered up and wearing a white veil"*. Angela's other recollections were of Christmas parties at the Epiphany, a wooden cross being carried to the top of the Beacon at Easter and the Nativity Plays. In one of the plays, The Story of Bethlehem, adult members of the congregation played most of the parts. Angela recalls that the real mother of the person playing Mary usually played the part of St Ann, the Virgin Mary's mother. On her copy of the script is written, *"Cecil Langford was one of the Shepherds"*.

Defeat had come perilously close but after a hard fought victory our way of life was preserved and peace returned to Europe in May 1945 and later in the year in the Far East.

Writing in the Church Magazine in 1949, Horace Keast refers to Two Cornish Parishes – St Agnes and Falmouth. The part relating to St Agnes is included here.

"...in the heyday of the last century, the township of St Agnes, on the north coast of Cornwall, was a thriving centre of one of the tin mining districts of the Duchy. The local industry prospered and the little cove of Trevaunance was converted into a harbour, with a granite breakwater, for the ships which called on the tin mining business. But came the slump in the Cornish tin mines – derelict pits and engine houses, mass unemployment, wide scale emigration – an altered pattern of life in the little Cornish township. Tin mining, apart from a few brave ventures, has now given place to basic agriculture, together with catering for summer visitors and once again St Agnes is meeting with a degree of prosperity...the Church of St Agnes...has a large and faithful congregation and its interior is a place of rare beauty. As one enters the south door there is a rugged stone altar of the Chapel of All Souls at the west end of the Church. Not far away is a real children's corner - a place where children can come and sit and read - and say their prayers. Then there is the lovely Church of Our Lady with its comely shrine of the Blessed Virgin. Votive lights burn before the statue. There is an impressive Chapel of the Blessed Sacrament where the Most Holy Sacrament is reserved for those unable to come to communion at the time of Mass. A noble rood beam, with crucifix and statues of Our Lady and St John, spans the chancel entrance. And then there is the massive stone high altar with its impressive canopy – the altar which is indeed the focal point of the Church.

Mass is said daily in this Church of the small township of St Agnes and on Sunday mornings there is the Parish Mass with a splendid congregation, men as well as women and children. The cycle of traditional observances of the Church Year are fully observed – Christmas with its joyful Midnight Mass, followed by Epiphany, with its own local and majestic Nativity Play, written and produced by the Parish Priest, Fr G H Barnicoat. Candlemass and Ash Wednesday, Rogationtide procession of blessing, Holy Week and Easter – they are all observed with fitting solemnity by the Cornish parishioners of St Agnes. The Church has been served by a succession of devoted Parish Priests and the fine traditions of the Parish are being both upheld and consolidated by Fr Barnicoat. Mention must be made, however, of one of the former vicars – the Revd W H Browne, now at rest. He was really the priest who laid the foundations of the Catholic Revival in this Cornish township and his memory is still held in high regard by all the parishioners – non-conformists as well as Church people, the rood is his memorial in the Parish Church."

In May 1951 the Revd Guy Barnicoat recorded the centenary year of St Agnes Church with an article in the Church Magazine. He starts by saying, *"When one sits down to write about something that only occurs once in a hundred years, it is difficult to know where to begin; it is a thing that one does only once in a lifetime".*

He reflects on the origin of the Church buildings at St Agnes. *"On May 28th 1851 the present, the third Church of St Agnes, was dedicated by Henry, Lord Bishop of Exeter, to the glory of God and under the patronage of St Agnes, Virgin and Martyr. It was a great day for St Agnes. For centuries we had been a chapelry under the Mother Church of Perranzabuloe and many things, such as the right of burial, rankled in the minds of St Agnes people.*

Of the first Church we know nothing. When St Piranus preached at Perranporth, then known as Tywarnhayle, in about 430 AD, the men of St Agnes, also known as Tywarnhayle, only five miles away, would certainly have gone out to hear him, if he had not visited them himself. A Christian community would have been formed and the first Church or Chapelry of St Agnes built, quite a small and simple building. We know that a church existed in St Agnes in 1331, for Bishop Grandison's register of that year gives an account of a visitation of St Agnes Chapel, which appears to have been sadly neglected.

This Chapel was pulled down at the end of 1482 and the second Church was completed in 1484 and consecrated and dedicated to the honour of Almighty God, in the name of St Agnes, as a daughter Church to Perranzabuloe.

In 1846, after being connected for over five hundred years with Perran, St Agnes became an independent Parish with the Reverend A A Vawdrey as its first Vicar. According to the Exeter Diocesan Registers the Order in Council whereby the Parish of St Agnes was severed from Perranzabuloe is dated 25th February 1846. To celebrate its emancipation from Perran the parishioners of St Agnes pulled down the second Church of 1484 and built the present Church, although much of the old material was used. The foundation stone was laid on August 22nd 1848 and was completed and the first service held on Tuesday July 24th 1849. It was not dedicated however until two years later, when presumably the Lord Bishop of Exeter visited Cornwall for he dedicated the Parish Church of Charlestown the same week.

So although we are about to celebrate a Centenary, it is with full and thankful hearts that we praise God for over six hundred years, and quite probably twice that number of centuries, of religious life and worship in a Church of St Agnes. It is something to be proud of but at the same time it is a tremendous responsibility. In a Church in this place the faith has been handed down and the Sacraments administered through the centuries to countless thousands. Are we adding our contribution to the spiritual life of the Church and its witness to all mankind? Are we maintaining and consolidating what has been handed down to us since the days when St Piranus landed on our shores? Let us rejoice but at the same time let us be fully conscious of our Christian calling and responsibilities."

The Revd Barnicoat then talks about the events of the Feast of Dedication week and to request gifts of money for improvements to the Church. He continued, *"We require at least £500 and once we begin on the Sanctuary a great deal more for the Sanctuary as it is, is quite unworthy of a beautiful Church like ours. I shall be sitting in the Lychgate, or (if wet) in Church on Monday May 28th...to receive gifts and hope you will bring yours then.*

In closing may I add how proud I am to be the sixth incumbent of St Agnes Parish Church and the successor of a long line of Parish Priests.

We send greetings to all who have left St Agnes and friends of our Parish Church. May God bless you all and give you a very happy Festival.

Your affectionate friend and Vicar, Guy H Barnicoat."

The programme of events for the Centenary Celebrations lasted from the 27th of May to the 4th of June 1951 and included many religious services and pageants. There was a dance in the Church Hall, an organ recital, a pageant, a garden party with St Agnes Prize Silver Band, sports and games for the children and, of course, the Vicar sitting in the Lychgate.

David Docking leading a Church procession circa 1950s

In 1958 the Church Magazine reported on the Sunday school outing. *"What a glorious day we had! We left St Agnes in pouring rain and it rained most of the way to St Ives but as we arrived, at 10.45am, the clouds rolled away and for practically the whole of the day we had brilliant sun. At lunchtime we could see the rain over St Agnes and thought how you must be pitying us. But it was wasted sympathy as we were getting more and more sunburnt. The tide was right and we were able to enjoy the beach all the morning. In the afternoon some went to sea and others went shop gazing. Everyone went home happy having had a wonderful time."*

1958 – The Revd Guy Humphrey Barnicoat resigned his position as Vicar of St Agnes and following this decision he penned a letter for the Magazine.

"Dear Friends,

    This is a sad letter to write, as saying goodbye at all times is a melancholy business but even more so after twenty-one years. Also, it is the end of my active ministry.

    I am leaving the most beautiful and homely Church in Cornwall and the most delightful people to live and work with. But for all of this I go with thanksgiving in my heart that I have been permitted to minister to St Agnes for so long in your Church. For it is your Church. A Parish Priest is called to minister in a certain Parish but it is not his Church. It is the Church of the place; the Parish Church of the people of that place and its welfare depends entirely upon them. Parish Priests come and go but the people of the place go on…I am deeply grateful to all Church workers in whatever capacity; for their co-operation and help. They have been wonderful.

    St Agnes and its welfare will always be in my prayers and we go with the happiest memories.

    Yours affectionately,   Guy H Barnicoat."

A later insertion in the Church Magazine suggested that the Revd Barnicoat had become a tad impatient with his bosses. *"I simply cannot understand why no appointment has been made to this Living. I wrote and asked the Bishop's permission to resign in February. He at once informed the Registrar and I signed and handed in the Deed of Resignation on February 26th, five months ago, and still the Chapter has not made any appointment. I am very anxious that there shall not be a long interregnum between the time I leave and the induction of the new incumbent. However, we must be patient and wait."*

Farewell presentation to the Revd Guy Barnicoat - Dora Barnicoat, Roderick Dibbs (Church Warden), the Revd Guy Barnicoat, William Andain (Church Warden) and Miss King (photo by Ken Young)

In the winter of 1958 a Youth Dance was held every month in the Church Hall. The charge was sixpence (2.5p). The Vicar said, *"We are not out to make a profit but to pay our way. We are very grateful to members of the Women's Fellowship who run the refreshments and make other arrangements and Alan Thomas is a very efficient MC. The attendance is always very good and these dances are much appreciated and enjoyed."*

1959 – The Revd Francis Ambrose Sadler was appointed Vicar of St Agnes.

Revd Sadler with pipe

In 1962 Mr Andain and Mr Dibbs were re-elected to act as Church Wardens. At the same meeting, *"...it was agreed to proceed with the ordering of an oil-fired boiler for the Church heating".*

Just a year later the Vicar wrote, *"I have had to accept the resignation as Vicar's Warden of Mr Andain. I did this with the greatest regret though understanding and approving of his reason for tendering it."* Mr Andain had held the position for fourteen years. The Vicar continued, *"In his place I have invited Mr Harry Stowell and I am happy to say that he has accepted".*

    The reference to the Vicar's Warden refers to a now discontinued practice where the Vicar appoints a warden of his choice and the congregation elects the other.

Sunday school teacher Mavis Johns with her class in the 1960s.
Girls left to right: Ruth Oliver, Jane Gambie, Sarah-Jane Docking, Liz Glover, Suzanne Russell, Becky Glover, Pam Nankivell and Mary Oliver
Boys left to right: Tim Nankivell, Nigel Russell, Robin Williams, David Stevens, Michael Thomas and Stephen Lake

It was the end of an era at the nearby Epiphany Home when in 1967 it passed from the Sisters of the Epiphany to Cornwall County Council. The Vicar explained, *"This is solely due to the fact that the Community cannot any more spare Sisters for the work they have done here for nearly 100 years and is concentrating on the special work at the Convent in Truro and St Michael's Retreat House there. This is indeed a milestone in the history of St Agnes which will seem most strange without the familiar and loved presence of the Nuns in its midst. Coming right home, this absence of the Sisters will have its effect on the attendance at the daily Mass in our Church and we must face this and do our utmost to see that this daily worship goes faithfully on."*

Mr W Garfield Stevens was appointed Organist and Choir Master in 1967; he replaced Mr A G S Blatchford who had served in that position for thirty years. Becky Clarke recalled her time in the choir and Mr Blatchford's ruling that lady members had to sit in the Lady Chapel rather than in the choir pews.

The 1967 Rogation procession moving along Trevaunance Road to a nearby garden for the springtime blessing of the crops of the field and the sea (photo by Ken Young)

The Revd Sadler with the Church Servers and Choir circa 1970

Writing in the Church Magazine in 1972 the Vicar, the Revd Francis Sadler, said, *"The list of incumbents, since we became an independent parish, is not long, your present parson being number eight"*. This is interesting as according to our count he was number seven! Did he miscount or is there something that we haven't found?

1972 – The Revd Francis Ambrose Sadler resigned his position as Vicar of St Agnes.

1973 – The Revd Alfred Michael Williamson was appointed Vicar of St Agnes. He was a Redruth man who for about ten years previously had been the Vicar at St George's Church in Truro.

In 1979 the Church Choir enthused about their annual outing. *"We left St Agnes at 9.00am calling at the Jamaica Inn for coffee, then on to Golitha Falls where we had a beautiful walk through the woods by the river. Our next call was Cremyll which we reached at lunchtime. Our next stop was Cawsand which we found very cold and windy and by the time we reached Seaton it was raining. We came home by the coast road, the scenery was lovely. We finally stopped (as always) at Lanivet for fish 'n' chips. We arrived home about 9.00pm having thoroughly enjoyed our day."*

The first service of Nine Lessons and Carols was held on the 3rd of January 1982 when various village organisations took part in the readings.

At the 1982 Church meeting it was reported that the three Fellowships were flourishing. The Sunday school was a hive of activity and well supported and the Youth Fellowship had superseded the Junior Church on Sunday mornings. (Church Magazine April 1982)

1987 – The Revd Alfred Michael Williamson resigned his position as Vicar of St Agnes in October and the Church Wardens included this piece in the Magazine.
"Dear Friends,
With great regret we shall be saying goodbye to Father Michael and Wendy this month and wishing them bon voyage; a happy holiday with their daughter and family in Sydney and God's richest blessings on their new work in the Diocese of Perth, Australia…We give thanks to Almighty God for their fourteen years of devoted ministry in St Agnes, for their hospitality, guidance, loyalty and leadership at all times. We shall miss them both very much and look forward to hearing from them when they have time to write…In order to maintain services during the interregnum we have been in contact with the Rural Dean, Father Ken Rogers…We are pleased to report that Father Wynford Phillips is willing to do all he can to look after the Parish while we are without a priest."
The West Briton Argus reported that the Revd Williamson was swopping his seaside parish for one in the Australian Anglican Church – a sheep and wheat-farming community.

1988 – The Revd Michael John Adams was appointed Vicar of St Agnes.

St Agnes Feast Week is an annual event and in 1993 this report appeared in the Church Magazine.
"As you are well aware the Feast of St Agnes falls on the 21st January. This year we begin our Feast Week celebrations with a concert in the Church by the Mevagissey Male Voice Choir and on Tuesday, in the Church Hall there will be a Feast Week Social.
The actual Feast of St Agnes will be marked by a special Feast Service when our Guest Preacher will be The Venerable Rodney Whiteman, the Archdeacon of Bodmin.
The now traditional Children's Disco will be held on Friday and junior Church Club members will have free entrance but there is a charge of 50p for all others. Later that evening, at 7.30pm, the Feast Whist Drive will be held in the Church Hall. I know that Donald Blight, who kindly arranges all our whist drives, would be pleased to see new players and would also accept gifts for the prize table.
Feast Week closes with a Young People's Service of Prayer and Praise. Do please help us to maintain the tradition…"

13th September 1988 - Trevor Cowl (Church Warden), The Very Revd David Shearlock (Dean of Truro), The Right Revd Peter Mumford (Bishop of Truro), The Revd Father Michael Adams (Newly appointed Vicar of St Agnes), Rainsford Hocking (Crucifer), The Venerable Arnold Wood (Archdeacon of Cornwall) and Miss Ethel Haydon (Church Warden).

Kay Adams penned this report for the Magazine in 1993. *"Once again a band of intrepid walkers set off from the Beacon car park to walk the 16.5 mile route on the Truro Trek from St Agnes to Truro Cathedral. Some 28 of us began the walk and all but four completed the whole route although one did do half of it in a pushchair – but then she was only five!*

We were lucky with the weather which was warm with a pleasant breeze blowing to cool us down on the long hikes up the hills…Having set off rather earlier this year we were expecting to reach the Cathedral in plenty of time for the Service, essential this year as several of the children, organised by Helen Benney, were taking part in it…Hopefully we have raised well over £100 for the 'Save the Children Fund'.

We all spent a very enjoyable day and the degree of support and encouragement given by everyone was a pleasure to behold."

In 1994 a group of Church walkers repeated the walk and Kay Adams wrote of, *"No accidents but for one or two sore feet, plenty of muddy clothes and a strong desire to have a long, hot bath"*. The £150 raised was for the Save the Children Fund.

In 1995 RAF veterans gathered at the airfield (formerly RAF Perranporth) to remember their comrades who died there during the Second World War. The Royal British Legion paraded on the runway and the Revd Michael Adams (St Agnes) and the Revd Antony Wright (Perranporth) conducted a service. Mount Charles Band and the Royal British Legion took part in the march past. Group Captain David Green (retired), founder and chairman of the Spitfire Society, unveiled a plaque which read, *"In memory of those who lost their lives flying from RAF Perranporth and to commemorate all those who served here from 1941 to 1945".*

In December 1998 the Revd Michael Adams, Vicar at St Agnes Parish Church, officiated at the burial of the remains of the crew and passengers of the Packet Ship Hanover. A small mahogany coffin contained about 100 human bones, recovered by Colin Martin and his team during the salvage of the Packet Ship. A slate plaque read, *"In Remembrance of The Hanover Paquet - Captain Joseph Sherburn his crew and passengers who lost their lives sailing from Lisbon to Falmouth on 3rd December 1763".* (Jericho to Cligga)

1999 – The Revd Michael John Adams resigned his position at St Agnes on his appointment as Vicar of Newquay. In 2003 he was made an Honorary Canon of Truro Cathedral taking the Stall of St Conan.

2001 – The Revd Alan George Bashforth was appointed Vicar of St Agnes.
 Alan recalled his induction on the 29th of April 2001 with a smile. It is traditional for the new Vicar to ring the bells but at that time they were silent and undergoing repair. He was handed a drumstick with which to ring a solitary bell and it seems that the number of rings is meant to signify the period of incumbency. Having struck six times he drew back for the seventh but as he did so the head of the drumstick flew off. This must have caused some amusement at the time but now that six years have elapsed he wishes to record that he has no intention of sticking to the principle.

The Revd Alan Bashforth

The 150 Years Anniversary took place in 2001 and was by way of a Floral Celebration. The programme stated, *"To celebrate this occasion, each window has a display depicting events of local interest during this time"*.

Memorial Chapel – by the Royal British Legion.
Bell Tower – Model of Church by Bill Cheshire.
Children's Corner – by the County Primary and Sunday school.
Agriculture – by the Village Garden Association.
Trevaunance Harbour – by the RNLI.
Mining – by Breannick Women's Institute.
Sports & Leisure – by the Short Mat Bowls Club.
Doctors – by Floral Art.

In 2005 Becky Clarke (née Glover) was made a Church Warden and joined Carol Buscombe (née Bunt) who had held the post for a couple of years. Prior to them Mollie Whitworth (née Mitchell) and Jennifer Selvey had held the posts.

In January 2007 the Anglican and Methodist Churches of St Agnes held two combined morning Covenant services – one in each building - to which over 100 people attended.

Over the years the Church has held many social activities such as the twice-yearly quiz organised by Alan and Lis Bashforth. The Church Hall is filled with wanabee quiz champions with the pasty supper and bring your own drinks as an additional feature.

Other Churches in the Area

The Church of St Peter at Mithian.
The Gazetteer of Cornwall 1884 states that Mithian is, *"An ecclesiastical Parish formed in 1846 from the Parish of St Agnes, Kea, Kenwyn, and a portion of the ecclesiastical Parish of Chacewater. The Church of St Peter is situate in the centre of the Parish, 4 miles northeast of Redruth, and consists of a chancel, nave, transept, porch, and a handsome tower and spire containing one bell."*

The original name of the new Parish was Silverwell, but owing to the diminishing importance of that village due to mine closures the name was changed to Mithian. Having found by measurement the centre of the Parish, the Revd Lord decided to build the Church on that spot.

It seems that at a late stage in its construction, there were still lingering concerns regarding its location and the Revd Alfred Lord wrote an open letter to the Royal Cornwall Gazette explaining the decision. He considered that he had built it in a position that made it within reach of the whole of the Parish which building it in the sheltered hamlet of Mithian or the thickly inhabited village of Blackwater would not. He went on to say that it was his eventual wish to build small Chapels at Mithian and Blackwater. (Mithian)

Because of falling numbers the Church ceased to meet for worship in December 2006.

Meeting House at Peterville
The surf shop in Peterville has had many uses including as a garage but it was as a Church that it was first built – in 1779. The Revd Thomas Wills was the curate at St Agnes during the 1770s and the Bizley's state that he, *"Did great work in St Agnes, his church being often filled from door to door"*. It seems that in 1774 he married Selina Wheeler, a near relative of the Countess of Huntingdon and she persuaded him to leave St Agnes to take charge of her dissenting chapels in various parts of the country. He left in 1779 but before he did he financed the erection of a meeting house for the Connection at Peterville *"...for the benefit of the small flock of followers he was leaving behind"*. The meeting house was licensed on the 18th November 1780 by the Dean and Chapter of Exeter Diocese as being, *"set apart for a place of Religious Worship in which a congregation do design to meet as Protestant Devotees"*. (A copy of the licence and of the history of this building by Bill Morrison is included in the 3rd Journal of the St Agnes Museum Trust)

Old Church in Mithian
In his paper of July 1965 John King of Mithian, wrote, *"An ancient church, now a farm building, is situated at the western approach to the village (Mithian). Little is known of its history but the present church, dedicated to St Peter, is some three miles distant."*

The Church of St John's at Mount Hawke
The ecclesiastical Parish of Mount Hawke was formed in 1846 out of areas taken from Perranzabuloe and Illogan. The Revd E M Hamilton had been the Curate at St Agnes and when the new Parish of Mount Hawke came into being he became its first Vicar.

One of Ashley Rowe's articles in The West Briton in 1958 states, *"A curious feature of the Extension movement of 1846 is that incumbents were appointed to the new districts and left to make their own arrangements for building a church and vicarage...the new incumbents seem to have been given a free hand; in fact, it was the only thing they were given!"*

Before the new Church was built a disused Congregational Chapel served as both schoolroom and church and it was 32 years before a church was built. Five incumbents held the living before the sixth, the Revd William Henry Allin, raised the necessary funds for the building work.

Ashley Rowe was clearly not impressed with the new church as he wrote, *"Mount Hawke cannot claim to have any architectural or aesthetic value. It is severely plain, entirely devoid of ornament. If a name must be given to the style it would be described as Early English. It consists of nave and chancel only, with a vestry at the east and a porch on the west end of the south side. There is a small bell turret at the west end of the building. It was definitely a case of 'cutting one's coat according to the cloth'. It has, however, the merit of being a local production; the architect was Charles Hancock of St Agnes and the builders were Mitchell and Langdon, also of St Agnes, together with Tamblyn of Redruth."*

The font was from the chapel at Trevaunance Manor – a mansion at St Agnes which was the home of a Roman Catholic family. It is said that Charles II sheltered there during the English Civil War but many large houses in Cornwall claim that distinction.

The Celtic Oratory at Chapel Porth

Chapel Porth has a connection with the ancient Church at St Agnes through its small Celtic Oratory, the ruins of which were visible as late as 1780. Close to this little cell was St Agnes Well. The Misses Quiller-Couch wrote in Ancient and Holy Wells of Cornwall that the well existed in an entire state until about 1820. Above it was a little Gothic edifice. *"...the destruction of the chapel and its well was affected by time and lack of faith and reverence. It is said that the principal depredators, who carried away the stone to build a hedge, said, when remonstrated with, 'What's the good of a well without any water?' The well had been drained by the delvings of the miners in a work below. Dr Dexter points out that here are many of the signs of a monastic enclosure or Lan-an oratory (Porth Chapel) built within view of the sea; a well (St Agnes Well); a stream (the Porth Chapel Stream) and a cross (Towan Cross at the head of the valley)."*

This cross has been lost, although it may still be hidden in the scrub ground near the Cross Roads. It is often a feature in Cornish villages to find a symbol of very early Christianity in the form of a Celtic cross, either in the churchyard, near to the south porch, or just outside the churchyard.

The Catholic Church

The Catholic Church at St Agnes is on Trevaunance Road, near Wheal Friendly. It was consecrated on the 15th of June 1958 and placed in the charge of the Redruth Priest.

A Roman Catholic Church was once located near Cliff Farm (behind Zion House) at Trevellas. It was a wooden building about 50 feet by 20 feet, light brown and with a niche in the front gable for an icon. John King wrote that Irish immigrants erected the Church in 1882. He said, *"The Trevellas Church closed in 1933. The congregation then went to the new church at Perranporth."*

In 1925 The Book of St Agnes said, *"Presumably there are a few Roman Catholics here as they have a little chapel at Trevellas, visited from time to time by a Priest".* The building was demolished in 1940 to make way for the airfield but by then it was being used as a tool shed. (Jericho to Cligga)

Methodist Chapels

John King wrote, *"A Methodist Society was formed at a very early date. A meeting house was erected before 1760. The first Chapel was built at Goonown in 1780*, in Goonown Lane. The present Chapel, in British Road* (often referred to as Big Chapel), *was built in 1860 in its own grounds and to seat 930 people. Near the northern entrance stands the War Memorial.* (*This date is uncertain and it may have been a few years later)

The Masonic Hall at Rosemundy was built in 1835 as a Chapel of the Methodist New Connection. The late William Booth, founder of the Salvation Army, preached there before the World Wide organisation was formed."

There were a number of Meeting or Preaching houses built in the late 1700s for those referred to as Dissenters. They were, of course, Christian but the members were said to be dissenting from the Church of England. Methodism in Cornwall grew rapidly but following Wesley's death in 1791 various offshoots were created and there was a proliferation in chapel building. Most were well attended but these divisions contributed to the eventual surplus of places of worship and of their subsequent conversion into dwellings. (Blackwater and its Neighbours)

The Buildings and Fabric of the Church

The First Church

We cannot be certain when the first Church was built at St Agnes or how many have stood on the present site but we have assumed the first building to be the one that was referred to in Bishop Grandisson's Register, in 1331, when St Agnes Chapel was described as *"Sadly neglected"*. It said, *"The clasps for the sacred books used in the services were broken, as were the Pixes for the Eucharist and the oils. The vessels for the incense were missing as were the bier for the dead and the pall. The tower bell was insufficient, the vestments were old and torn and the chapel walls and roof were unsound."* The parishioners were instructed to, *"Put their Chapel in order and to provide all things necessary for the celebration of Divine Service".*

The Second Church

The second Church was built in 1484, on the site of the earlier Church and it is said that the Church was then rededicated to St Agnes.

The Bishop decreed that a chaplain be maintained at St Agnes at the cost of the Vicar of Perranzabuloe. A house and stable was to be provided by the inhabitants who were required to maintain the, *"fabric of the chapel, its books and ornaments, seats and vestments and window; the vicar to maintain the chaplain's house, but to receive all mortuaries as usual".*

The historian Hals wrote, *"The Chapel was augmented and rebuilt of three roofs, as it now stands, by the charitable collections and the proper charge and cost of the inhabitants thereof in 1484, consecrated and dedicated to the honour of Almighty God, in the name of St Agnes, as a daughter Church to Perransand, by Dr Peter Courtenay, then Bishop of Exon".*

In Gilbert's book Cornwall it says, *"The Church is a decent edifice with a spire and bells and over the entrance to the west end are the arms of Tonkin cut in stone…Near the altar stands a marble monument inscribed to the Tonkin family, late of Trevaunance in this Parish. It has a long Latin inscription which has been lately published with Tonkin's notes in Carew's Survey of Cornwall, by Lord Dunstanville. In the middle of the south aisle is placed a marble tablet to the memory of G O C St Aubyn, who died April 7th 1776."*

During the early 1700s Thomas Tonkin of Trevaunance wrote an account of St Agnes: *"St Agnes is a daughter church to St Piran in the Sands…Formerly there was only a small chapel dedicated to this she saint; and the parishioners were obliged on the more solemn days…to resort to the said Mother Church, where was an aisle allotted to their use. But the people increasingly, drawn hither by the tin mines, and the Mother Church being at least seven miles distant from some parts of the parish, petitioned for leave to build a church here; which was accordingly granted them by Peter Courtney then Bishop of Exeter, on certain conditions contained in the same grant given at his Palace at Exon October 1st 1482."* He refers to these conditions as involving superstitious ceremonies and the building of a vicarage.

Tonkin continued, *"The Church, such as it is at present, was accordingly built and conse-crated and stands, I suppose, on the same ground on which was the former Chapel, about the middle of the before-mentioned little town, and of the parish, in a low situation, and near one half of the western end buried. It consists of a nave, two aisles, and a small tower with a spire, in which there are three bells; and it was at that time sufficient to contain all the inhabitants, which are now grown so numerous that there is at present as much need to enlarge the said church as formerly to build it."*

According to Tonkin the windows were paintings of the history of the life and martyrdom of St Agnes but these were mostly broken at the time of the Grand Rebellion – the English Civil War of 1642.

A painting by Edward Opie (1810-1894) provides us with a good impression of the building but it is suggested that it may have been drawn from memory as the east windows are not in the style of a 15th century church. Above the Church can be seen the roof of the Market House which stood on the site of the lychgate. The roof appears somewhat shorter than we believe the building to have been which may reinforce the view that the painting was undertaken from memory.

Tonkin refers to an application in 1712 to enlarge the Church. The design was approved by the Right Reverend Ofspring Blackall, Bishop of Exeter, who, *"Recommended it in a particular manner to the clergy of his Diocess to forward the contributions to so good a work. But,"* continued Tonkin, *"such hath been the iniquity of the times that nothing hath been hitherto done in it: only as a specimen of what was designed, the writer hereof hath built a small cross isle to the north, for the use of himself and family, and yielded up to the parish his ancient seats in the nave of the church".*

From a mining map of 1838 the length of the Church appears to be little more than the width but we cannot be sure of the accuracy of such a small-scale drawing. There is a projection to the north elevation and this may be Tonkin's cross aisle.

The churchyard was enlarged in 1717 and Thomas Tonkin wrote, *"To the south, a piece of land having been bought, for that purpose, of John Nance of Trengoffe Esq. and Chester Nance Esq. his son and heir apparent, by the writer hereof, in trust and for the use of the Parish; but the same having not been consecrated, few people care to have their friends buried therein".*

The suggested image of 1484 Church – a reproduction of a painting by Edward Opie

In 1816 the Church Authorities acquired some additional burial ground. The plot known as Slade's Meadow was situated between British Road and Rosemundy Hill; it was purchased for £255 from Olivie Prout. (Church Magazine 1925)

Dr John Wolcot died in 1819 and a simple cross was erected to his memory. This extraordinary man was a physician, took holy orders and, in 1778, turned to literature. He discovered John Opie, the

Cornish painter, from Trevellas. He took him to London where he became known as the *"Cornish Wonder"*. Dr Wolcot was a great satirist and wit who wrote under the nom de plume *"Peter Pindar"*.

The Third Church

Circa 1855 – The new Church nestling into the village

The existing Church was considered much too small for the congregation which had grown due to the vast mining activity in the Parish but although Bishop Blackall of Exeter approved an enlargement in 1714 the rebuilding did not take place for about 130 years. Whatever the reason for the delay, the Church was not completed until 1849.

Permission to, *"Take down and rebuild on the same spot a new Church,"* was said to be in celebration of emancipation from Perranzabuloe. Henry, Lord Bishop of Exeter, granted it on the 1st of October 1842 to the Perpetual Curate of the Parish Church and the parishioners of St Agnes.

James Piers St Aubyn (1815-1895) of London undertook the design. He was an architect with strong Cornish connections having been educated at Penzance Grammar School and related to the St Aubyns of St Michael's Mount.

On the 28th April 1848 the Royal Cornwall Gazette reported, *"A meeting of ratepayers was held at Pearce's Hotel on Tuesday last to empower the Churchwardens to borrow, agreeably to the provisions of an act passed in the reign of George III for the purpose of rebuilding the Parish Church. It was resolved to raise a loan of £500, which sum, with the donations promised, is said to be sufficient for the purpose. The old building is in a very dilapidated state, and will shortly be pulled down. The new Church is to be completed in about 18 months."*

On the 11th August 1848 the West Briton newspaper reported, *"An adjourned meeting of the Vestry of this Parish was held at Pearce's Hotel on Friday last. Mr Hitchens in the chair, when Mr Carne of Rosemundy, Churchtown, proposed that the Parish should confirm the borrowing of £500 at 5% from an insurance company in London, to be paid within five years for the rebuilding of the Church*

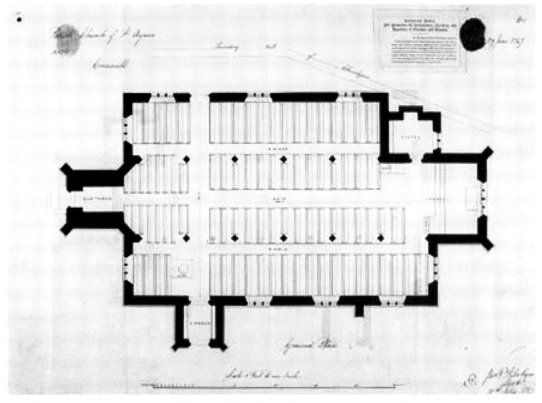

The floor plan of the proposed Church – the solid wall to the left of the vestry is now an arched opening containing the Blessed Sacrament Altar (Courtesy of Lambeth Palace Library)

and Mr Vawdry, the Vicar, having obtained the sum of £1,000, as he had promised in the early stage of the proceedings, he thought the Parish could not proceed under more favourable circumstances.

After some consultation the Churchwarden's proposition was carried by a large majority. Mr Norton then moved that a vote of thanks be tendered to Mr Carne for his indefatigable exertions in bringing the business to this issue, which was carried by acclamation.

A building committee was then proposed, consisting of six gentlemen, exclusive of the Vicar and Churchwardens, after which a vote of thanks to the Chairman was proposed by Mr R Norton Jnr, seconded by the Revd A A Vawdrey and carried unanimously. The committee met on Monday and having examined the tenders will immediately proceed to take down the old Church and shortly the foundation stone will be laid for the new edifice."

The original intention had been to raise the necessary funds by levy and permission was granted to set this at two shillings and sixpence (12½p) in the pound however but this was rescinded and a loan arranged.

Demolition began within a fortnight and by the 22nd August 1848, less than three weeks after the initial meeting at which it was agreed to start work, Archdeacon Preb. Phillpotts laid the foundation stone of the new Church. A considerable accomplishment and undoubtedly much quicker than would have been achieved in today's bureaucratically hindered climate.

Almost all of the old Church was demolished in the course of the work. Writing in The Book of St Agnes the Revd Browne said, *"The old materials were re-used and the building was considerably enlarged. Fortunately these 19th century vandals left the west wall of the Nave and the Tower standing and incorporated them into the new Church."* From this we can see that the increase in the length of the Church must have been to the east – Peterville end.

Less than a year later, on the 24th July 1849, the Church was opened for services and on the 28th May 1851, the new building of nave, with north and south aisles, was dedicated. An impressive timescale.

The new Church is in the style of the Decorated Period and the pillars supporting the arches are of St Stephen's stone – the roofs being of the open cradle pattern.

The St Agnes guide book of 1936 states that, *"Only two of the historical Tonkin monuments are left and these – one inside, bearing the arms of Hugh Tonkin impaling those of Vincent, the other outside, of his son impaling those of Kempe – are built into the wall of the Church, near the north door"*.

The Bishop of Exeter visited St Agnes in July 1877, to consecrate the new Mortuary Chapel and the Church of England portion of the Cemetery. He then went to Mount Hawke where he laid the foundation stone of the new church. (St Agnes 1001-1999)

The Hungry Man or *"Pore"* man's box – a carved and painted
wooden figure which supports the Elizabethan Alms Box;
this curious item is thought to have been transferred from the
1484 Church (Sketch by Alice Bizley)

Writing in the Church Magazine in 1972 the Vicar, the Revd Francis Sadler, said, *"The 'Poor Man' affixed to the westernmost pillar of the south arcade is a poor box believed to date from the days of Good Queen Bess. It is, of course, long pre-Welfare…in the days when the poor had very few entitlements and depended too much on the arbitrary charity of their 'betters'. We can be glad such a chancey system no longer obtains, in spite of some contemporary abuse of our better ways today."*

On the 5th of March 1903 the Royal Cornwall Gazette included a very detailed description of a new installation. *"A very handsome stained glass window has just been put in the north aisle of St Agnes Church. It consists of three lights and tracery.*

In the first light is represented the angel announcing to the holy women the Resurrection of our Lord. 'Come, behold the place where the Lord lay'. In the centre light is depicted our Lord coming out of the tomb and the soldiers who were left on guard. One of the latter is sleeping and the other is witness to the scene. The third light represents our Lord appearing to the disciples and the miraculous draught of fishes. In the tracery above these lights are the words, 'I am the Resurrection and the life'. At the base of the window is the following inscription: 'To the glory of God and in pious memory of Anna Twite who died 19th October 1902, aged 62, this window is inserted by her husband and sons'.

The designing and the executing of the entire window has been carried out by Mr Arthur L Moore of Southampton-row, London."

Two letters from the Revd Rudall to Mr Twite are lodged with the County Records Office. The first explained that, "A faculty is necessary before any alteration or addition to the fabric of the Church". The second says, "I have seen the sketch of the window which you propose to put in the Church in memory of Mrs Twite and like it very much".

The estimate for designing, executing and fixing the window at, "St Agnes, Scorrier, Cornwall," was £91.

In 1905 there was considerable damage to the walls when the Church spire was struck by lightening. A report in a local newspaper on the 16th of March 1905 stated

"Gale in the West - St Agnes Church Steeple Damaged
Struck by Lightning and Knocked out of Perpendicular.

About noon yesterday a torrent of rain and hail fell. A flash of lightning of blinding brilliancy was followed immediately by a thunderclap of tremendous force, reminding some of the noise made on the occasion of the dynamite explosion at Perranporth some years ago. The shock was so great that one person was knocked down, and others were almost thrown down. The greatest damage, however, was done to the steeple of the Parish Church. This was struck by the electric fluid, and about eight feet at the top of the steeple, in addition to the vane, was carried away. Nearly the whole of the debris fell upon the roof of the building. But this was strongly built, only a few comparatively small holes were made. Some of the granite stones were found inside the Church. The steeple appears to have been struck on the south-west side, as the coping around the steeple and on the top of the tower has been carried away in one place, and in others shaken and broken. There is also a place about six feet high in the lower part of the tower the stones of which have been loosened, and the whole steeple is considerably out of perpendicular. It will have to be taken down, unless a continuance of the stormy weather brings it down with a crash. One stone fell on the roof of Mrs Williams's house, which stands opposite the Church, and slightly damaged it; and glass in the windows of several houses was broken. On the north side of the Church one of the granite stones to which are fixed the ornamental railings was found to be broken, and the turf torn up near by, although no stone could be found near the spot. The railings escaped without damage, and no further damage was done, although a resident stated that it appeared to him that the lightning struck the road in the centre of the town.

Another correspondent states that several of the stones from the steeple were thrown a great distance, one going right through the roof of the Church and making a hole the size of a man's head. Another was found in a field nearly 200 yards away, and one struck the corner of Mrs Williams's grocer's shop and carried away a portion of the guttering and masonry, and damaged the window. The door of the tower was burst open, while an inner door leading into the steeple was shattered to fragments. The iron gate leading to the vicarage was also damaged. Mrs Lampshire, living in a house about fifty yards off, was using a knife when the flash occurred, and her arm was temporarily paralysed. Miss Langdon, living just across the road, was similarly affected, while using a fork. The Vicar (the Revd A Rudall) says he was sitting in his study at the time. He saw a globe of fire, and then heard an explosion, which disappeared in a blue flash. He then knew that something had been struck. At West Kitty Mine the lightning, which was followed by a blinding hail-storm, played up and down the steel cable at the shaft, and several of the miners working in the 110 fathom level and 100 fathoms in the stope were knocked down by the shock. A shock was also experienced at Wheal Friendly. At present what remains of the Church steeple has a decided list to the west, and has a very shaky appearance. The damage is estimated at several hundred pounds, but the edifice is insured."

This was clearly a major event in the village and must have been the topic of conversation for some time. Within a very short period action was being taken and on the 23rd of March 2005 the Royal Cornwall Gazette reported, *"A steeplejack arrived at St Agnes on Saturday afternoon, and removed the loose stones on the top of the steeple. He found it very difficult to find a firm hold for the cramps by which to hold the ladders, showing that the steeple had a greater shock than those who inspected it on Friday were prepared to admit. He, however, reached the top and threw down eight large stones which were very loose. He also gave it as his opinion that the steeple was unsafe, and that it would be dangerous to hold the usual service in the Church. The Vicar (the Revd Alfred Rudall) gave notice that the Church would be closed, and that the services would be held in the schoolroom. Inside the Church a large crack was observable in the arch nearest the tower in the north aisle, and it looked as if the arch had also been slightly shaken out of position. In some parts light could be seen between the boarding of the roof. The holes in the roof have been patched in order to keep out rainwater. The steeple was built by a man named Thomas Delbridge, and was generally admired for the very fine work that was put into it, and for being so true. The steeple was built in 1848 when the present edifice was erected, but the tower on which it rests was a part of the old Church, and is over four hundred years old."*

A couple of weeks later and it was still in the news and the Royal Cornwall Gazette report of the 6th of April 1905 stated, *"The taking down of the damaged steeple and a part of the battlement of the tower was completed on Wednesday last and this part of the Church now presents a very dilapidated appearance.*

The steeplejack, Mr Larkins, of Bow, London, has stated that the blow must have been of so tremendous force as there was not a sound joint to be found in the bottom of the steeple.

So badly was it shaken that it surprised him that the whole structure had not fallen. It made it difficult and dangerous to work with the bottom part so insecure.

The crack in one of the arches inside the Church he attributed to the falling of the vane and debris on the roof as it must have come down with great force."

Work was also carried out to the bells at this time and this is mentioned under the section entitled bell ringing.

The steeple showing the damage after the lightning strike in 1905

The tower without its steeple - note the iron standpipe and the railings later removed for munitions in the Second World War

The Royal Cornwall Gazette of the 24th of June 1909 reported, *"A new lighting and heating arrangement has been fixed at the St Agnes Church and the dedicatory service was conducted on Friday evening by the Lord Bishop of St Germans. Unfortunately something went wrong with the working of the system and the new lights could not be used. The firm in Devonport in reply to urgent telegrams promised to send someone to put the matter right but he had not turned up on Friday evening.*

The clergy present in addition to the Lord Bishop were the Revds A Rudall (Vicar), J C Barfett (Mount Hawke) and S Richards (Curate). The service was fully choral with Mr A W Gill of Truro at the organ and the choir ably rendered the anthem 'Thou wilt keep him in perfect peace'."

It seems that the churchyard was increased in size in 1909 by a gift of a piece of ground – from Mr Naylor Carne.

There are many features and artefacts of interest in the Church, several of them given by members.

Mrs Martin of Elm Villa donated the oak choir stalls in memory of her late husband, Thomas Martin (1830-1911), who had been a Church Warden for 34 years. The brass Angel Lecturn was in memory of William Naylor Carne who had regularly read the lessons. The parishioners presented the carved oak altar rails in 1922 in memory of the Revd Alfred Rudall. The Litany desk was in memory of Emma Eudey and given by her husband in 1923 and the two altar candlesticks were in memory of Mrs Jones.

There is a small Elizabethan Cover Paten, three inches in diameter which probably belonged to the Chalice at Perranzabuloe and became mixed when the livings were held together. It bears no marks but the Chalice has the mark of John Jons of Exeter. The Cover has a leaf ornamentation with a Tudor Rose design on the foot.

An interesting piece of the Church Plate has been lent to the Royal Institution of Cornwall and is exhibited in the County Museum in Truro. This is a flagon, made in 1710 and also given by John Worth to the Parish of St Agnes.

The Statue of Our Lady was designed by Miss Salusbury and dedicated by the Bishop on 27 January 1928 and there are several icons brought back from a pilgrimage to Constantinople (Istanbul) and the Holy Land by Mr Dowling and Mrs B M Josa in 1925.

On the south wall is a memorial to William Whitworth who died in 1917. He was the Parish medical practitioner for 37 years, one of a number of St Agnes doctors from the Whitworth family. The memorial also commemorates another member of this family of medical men, Captain H P Whitworth who was killed in October 1918 and is buried in Ypres. A simple wooden cross bearing his name is fixed to the splay of the window over the Memorial Chapel in the south-west corner of the Church. On the other splay of the same window is another soldier's cross to Private A Trounce of the 1st DCLI. The window is in memory of Thomas Oliver and Martha Prout who died in 1867.

On the south wall is a tablet, *"Sacred to the memory of John Luke of this Parish, many years Captain of the Gongo Soco and Bananal Gold Mines in Brazil, who died in Rio de Janiero, 22 March, 1850, aged 43 years"*.

The carved oak pulpit, designed by Edmund Sedding FRIBA, was in memory of Martin and Nanny Hitchens and presented by their children in 1914. In 1972 the Revd Sadler described a pulpit as, *"An elevated platform from which the better to read or speak to a large number of people in a large building. It is therefore an entirely practical object."* He went on to say, *"Our particular pulpit is carved and ornate...Traditionally, pulpits are on the north side of the central aisle, the north being those parts where heathen darkness was held to prevail, hence also the reading of the liturgical Gospel from the north end of an altar."*

The pulpit carved with the figure of St Agnes and
emblems of The Passion with the newly created
Sacrament Altar in the background

St Agnes is fortunate in still having its Celtic Cross. At some time it was mutilated by having one projecting portion of the head cut off in line with the shaft; and the upper part straight across at the top.

Writing in The Book of St Agnes in 1925 the Revd Browne said, *"The War Memorial, an old Cornish Cross which was formerly a stone to rest coffins on, stands by the main gate to the Churchyard, it is of a peculiar shape and stands five feet four inches high".*

1905 - The Celtic Cross in its old position by the main gate - could the white patch on the ground to the left have been its original position when it was used as a resting place for coffins?

A G Langdon, in his book Old Cornish Crosses, deduces that the St Agnes Cross is a wheel cross with rude Celtic ornament on both sides and that it is probably 8th century since manuscripts of that period contain ornamentation of a similar nature.

In 1951 an article in the Church Magazines records the resiting. *"The Celtic Cross, which has stood for many years in the road beside the Lychgate, has now been moved to its proper place, near the south door of the Church. When the original site of a cross is not known, this should be its position according to a competent authority on these matters. It looks most imposing in its new position and can be seen by all. In its old place, many did not even know that it existed."*

The mutilated head of the Celtic Cross

The High Altar was constructed in 1924 and described in the Church Magazine. *"Our new High Altar, 8ft long, built of granite blocks and was generously given by Mr J Hitchens. It once formed part of the harbour pier and has been in the sea for about 140 years. It was consecrated by the Bishop on March 27th at a solemn Sung Mass. The Bishop was the celebrant and was assisted by Fathers Nash, Trewhella and the Vicar. There was a large congregation and 68 communicants."*

The organ was originally located at the east end of the north aisle, where the Chapel for the Blessed Sacrament now stands. The original floor plan shows the wall here to be solid but an arched opening was formed either when the Church was built or when the organ was installed in 1881.

Hele & Co of Plymouth built and installed the organ and despite our efforts we have been unable to determine how music was produced before then. Clive Ellison, the current organist, says that it has undergone a number of changes over the years but that it has always had two-manual keyboards.

Sometime around 1931 the organ was renovated and raised into an organ loft. A Sacristy was then formed below but because of limited height the organ pipes had to be cut and mitred to suit the slope of the roof. At one time the organist was concealed by a set of wooden pipes which seem to have been for decoration only; these were removed when the organ underwent a re-build in 1965. A new mixture stop was installed during the 1970s, paid for by Mrs Sadler, the Vicar's wife.

Clive Ellison became the organist in the 1990s and is well known for his recitals; he has worked for a number of organ builders and now repairs and tunes pianos.

The relocation of the organ provided space for the creation of the Chapel for the Blessed Sacrament which utilises the old High Altar, a delightful piece constructed of oak wreckage raised to the required level by the addition of new wooden blocks. The canopy was added at a later date. The stained glass window nearby is in memory of Anna Twite who died on the 19th October 1902.

The Chapel for the Blessed Sacrament where the organ was once located - the Statue of the
Sacred Heart is to the left

Circa 1930 - The Lady Chapel at the east end of the
south aisle; the stained glass window is in memory of
John James Halls who died in 1860

The Church once owned a Tazza cup, presented to the Parish of St Agnes by John Worth, a wealthy landowner of Tremough, near Penryn, a Justice of the Peace in three reigns and Sheriff of Cornwall in 1711. It was six inches in diameter, one inch deep and richly ornamented both on the stem, the base and in the centre of the bowl; it was made in 1579. There are only two other churches in Cornwall which possess Tazza cups - at Poughill and Mabe. (Portrait of a Village Church)

When a similar item was sold for £21,000 in 1969 the St Agnes one was immediately placed in a bank strongroom and insured against fire and theft. The risk of displaying it in the Church was considered to be too great and a decision was taken that it should be sold and the proceeds used to repair and re-hang the bells.

At a meeting of the Consistory Court at Truro on the 10th November 1971 the Chancellor of the Diocese gave judgement that the petitioners had narrowly convinced him of their need for necessary work on the Church and its other buildings and he gave his approval to its sale. He specified that it should by sold by Christies, that the Diocesan Board of Finance should invest the proceeds and that the interest should go to the St Agnes PCC to form the basis of a fabric fund devoted exclusively to the upkeep of the Church and its buildings.

At the sale in November 1972 the cup sold for £9,000 which was described as *"A very disappointing result"*. The net proceeds amounted to £7,482 and this figure, rounded up to £7,500, was invested and the Church received the first dividend in October 1973.

It seems that the Tazza cup then passed through the hands of several dealers, was exhibited at the Victoria and Albert Museum and eventually purchased by the Cecil Higgins Art Gallery at Bedford for £16,000. It was later exhibited at the International Art Treasures Exhibition at Bath.

A memorial plaque was erected to John Worth Esq. and erected on the south wall with a picture of the Tazza cup beneath it.

In 1925 the Church Magazine referred to a wish to purchase a stained glass window. *"Miss Salusbury, the stained glass window artist of St Agnes and London, has painted a beautiful lancet window of St Agnes. A wish has been expressed that it should be secured for our Church. Canon Cooper, Chancellor of Truro Cathedral, and Mr R Wheatly ARIBA have inspected it and strongly advise this to be done. The cost is £30. Miss L Tremeane of the Russettings, St Agnes, has kindly consented to act as Treasurer and all contributions for this purpose should be given to her. A recent visitor to St Agnes has opened the Fund by giving 10/- (50p) in appreciation of St Agnes and its Church."*

The east window is a memorial to Mr and Mrs William Carne who, said John King, *"Generously helped the restoration in 1848".*

In 1927 an electricity supply was installed at Wheal Kitty Mine and three years later it came to the Church, at a cost of £103. 17s.

In 1927 the Revd W H Browne wrote in the Monthly Magazine about the mortuary chapel in the old churchyard – opposite the Railway Inn. *"This Chapel which is used as a mortuary chapel for those who have unfortunately lost their lives by accident, while they await inquest, is on consecrated ground and is itself consecrated. It has always grieved me to see one of its walls which abuts on Vicarage Road used as a public billposting station. It does not seem reverent and seemly to so use this building.*

I have hesitated to move in this matter because I understand that this billposting has been going on for some 40 years or more and some people seem to think that the public has acquired a prescriptive right to continue doing so.

I have submitted the legal question to the Registrar of the Diocese and the Bishop's legal adviser and I am advised that the law is quite plain that no such prescriptive right can be acquired.

In conversation with several old residents of the Parish, who opinions I respect, and who are by no means all churchmen, I am told the feeling and religious sentiment of the St Agnes people would be in favour of doing away with what is now an ugly eyesore. I do not wish to take any drastic action in this matter but I should like to ask the billposters not to paste any more notices and to let the kindly wind and rain do the rest."

The Monthly Magazine in 1928 refers to the discovery of dry rot. *"We have a lot of this in the Church and not only in the pulpit is it found but it abounds in the pews. It will be our wisdom to combat it whenever we get an opportunity by replacing the flooring with concrete. We have done this in the War Memorial Chapel, where the floor was one mass of it. In course of time the flooring of the whole Church must be done otherwise it will spread upwards and the roof may be attacked."*

In the Magazine in January 1929 the Vicar writes, *"...but an urgent need is to track out and destroy the dry rot in the Church. We have made a beginning in the south aisle and that beginning has shown us the necessity for really drastic measures if we are to prevent it attacking all the woodwork and possibly the roof too. The north and south aisles will have to have the rest of the pews removed and the floor filled up with concrete. It will mean disturbing the accustomed sitting place of many people but I am sure that they will understand the absolute necessity of the work if we are to avoid an enormous expense in the future. So far we have seen no trace of the dry rot in the centre of the Nave and if we can prevent it travelling there these pews need not be disturbed. It is very unfortunate but our duty is to do all we can to preserve intact, what we have inherited, for future generations."*

In 1931 the story rumbled on, *"The south aisle of the Church will be taken in hand very shortly. The benches will have to be replaced by chairs. We are wondering if our congregation will give* the chairs. They will come to about 10/- or 11/- each (50p or 55p). We want them to be a little more comfortable than the few chairs which are already in the Church, more comfortable that is both to kneel at and sit on. Two have already been promised, we want about 50 for the aisle."

The Royal Cornwall Gazette of the 8th of July 1931 included the following report. "The interior of St Agnes Parish Church will shortly undergo alteration. The benches in the north and south aisles are to be removed on account of the appearance of dry rot. This woodwork has been in its present position since the Church was re-built in 1847-8. The Church authorities are to provide chairs instead of benches but the benches in the centre will remain. The re-seating of the south aisle is to be proceeded with at once."

A 1932 edition of the Magazine states, "How you all must be heartily sick of this rot!! We have done the south aisle and re-seated it with chairs. The work has been beautifully done and the woodblock floor adds a charm to the Church. It shows us something of what the Church will look like when it is all done in the same way. There will be a dignity about it which is quite unexpected. And what a splendid response has been made to the Vicar's appeal for chairs to be given. One member of the congregation said, 'Our family is three in number, of course we will pay for the three chairs we shall want to sit on and we will give one for the stranger also'. That is the spirit to show and it is just in an emergency like this that St Agnes shows at its best and when it does that St Agnes cannot be beaten. Thank God the dry rot is confined to the floor and has not spread upwards to the congregation and the chairs are good too, they are the very same make and design that is being used to re-seat St Paul's Cathedral in London. St Agnes must always have the best, must it not?"

Later in 1932 the Revd Browne outlines the progress in the Magazine. "The relaying of the floor of the Church has provided us with many exciting thrills during the past three weeks.

While preparing the floor for the concrete bed it was noticed that a wall was running along the nave – between two of the pillars. On further examination it was found that this wall extended on both sides forming an oblong which might well have been the location of the old Church building which existed before the one built in 1484.

We then tried to find the eastern wall of this Church and found a wall about three feet west of the Chancel step. We cleared the earth away from the outside of the wall and found that for four feet downwards the stones had been pointed and showed signs of having been weathered for a very long time. This seemed to be the east end of the Church but on clearing away the earth on the other side we found that it was not the wall of a building at all but a retaining wall which in the long distant past must have been east of the old Church.

In the south-west corner a 15th century base of one of the pillars was unearthed, resting, no doubt, on the original floor of the 15th century Church, some four feet below the level on which the 19th century Church was built. Crossing the Nave were dwarf walls which were very puzzling. Between these walls and the floor we removed was a space which was filled with earth which contained a large quantity of human bones and on this again were dwarf walls which had carried the floor which we had to remove.

It looked as if further excavation would reveal the floor and walls of the first of the churches which is known to have existed on this spot and, possibly, may have been the original Celtic Church which again may have been the one converted from the old pagan fire worshippers' temple as Dr Dexter thought possible.

What other revelations of carving or altars may have been revealed we know not. If all had gone well we had thoughts of a crypt under the new floor of which we should have been proud. However, on further examination we came across vaults which had been built on the old floor and these vaults still contained bodies in a state of dissolution. The work was stopped at once, the ground filled in and now a bed of concrete (six inches thick) has been laid upon it, covering up for ever the secrets of the past.

So the net result is that we have found traces of three Churches all erected on the same site and we know roughly the level and size of these buildings.

When the vaults were built and who were buried in them we do not know but when the Church was practically re-built in 1848 the whole floor was raided in order that there might be room for the *vaults underneath. We only found one base of the pillars, no doubt the rest of them are still under-ground. The shafts and capitals of the old 15th century ones were re-erected on new bases in the 19th century restoration.*

One thought rises in my mind as I think of the hideous scene of corruption underneath. They must have been rich people who were so able to have these beautiful domed vaults prepared for their burial. No doubt they thought themselves very important folk but what right had they to intrude themselves into our midst today to spread their pestilential microbes amongst the living. At any rate they are now safely concreted down and the air is the better for it. It may be that the west end is in the same state and it behoves us to examine this too and to do the same thing there if necessary."

Lightning did strike in the same place twice when, in December 1929, the top of the spire, weighing over half a ton, was hurled ten feet to the east and smashed through the roof. It fell in one piece and is now placed outside the Church.

In 1934 a faculty was issued for a rood beam and a lychgate. (List of Faculties) The lychgate is a memorial to George Coulter Hancock presented by his son in 1934. A Market House was located there – a building which extended to the top of Town Hill. This was purchased by the Church on the 9th May 1894 for £250 and the building subsequently demolished.

In 1935 a faculty was issued dedicating a strip of land from the old churchyard to Cornwall County Council for road widening. (List of Faculties)

The Children's Corner is located in the north-west of the Church and in 1936 a faculty was issued for its re-construction and improvement. (List of Faculties) The stained glass window portrays the child Agnes holding a lamb in her arms - it was produced in 1936 by Miss Salusbury and dedicated to the memory of Maria Louisa Roffe. Theodora Salusbury moved to St Agnes in 1934 where she continued her career as a stained glass artist. She died in 1956 and left instructions to destroy the contents of her studio.

The Children's Corner with the stained glass window and the font which was moved to this position in the 1940s - on the right is a closer view of Miss Salusbury's window

In 1942 Truro Rural District Council issued a notice which said that on or after the 15th November the iron railings around the graves would be removed (for the war effort). The Magazine states, *"We part with them willingly for the purpose for which they are required and feel that the graves will look much better without them. With regard to the front of the Church facing the road, we hope that when the railings are gone people will not walk upon the grass and we especially appeal to the children not to run over it and play there."*

In 1947 the Church Magazine referred to the War Memorial Tablet. *"A sub-committee was appointed by the Parochial Church Council to carry out the work of adding the names of those who died in the Second World War 1939-1945 to the tablet behind the Memorial Altar. The Committee met on September 9th and decided to accept the plan of Mr Anthony Hawkey. As soon as a faculty has been obtained from the Chancellor an order will be placed for the carrying out of the work. A drawing of the proposed enlarged tablet will shortly be placed in the Church with a box for donations. As the names of all those who died in the Parish will be inscribed a public collection will be made and the Committee hopes that the Church organisations will help in this collection. The aim is to have the work complete by Remembrance Sunday, November 9th, but under present conditions, this may not be possible. We hope that everybody will give liberally towards this permanent memorial in the Parish Church to those who died in the service of their Country."*

The font is in Catacluse stone and is thought to have been transferred from the 1484 Church. In 1943 a faculty was issued for moving it from the south-west corner, by the main entrance, to the north-west corner of the Church. (List of Faculties)

The War Memorial – previously the location of the All Souls' Chapel - note the font before it was moved to the north-west corner of the Church

The next three pictures are from different dates but grouped together for comparison purposes. They are taken from similar positions - along the Nave towards the High Altar. The first is in circa 1912 before the pews were replaced by chairs - the organ in its original position is visible to the left.

Circa 1955, chairs have now replaced the pews and the Rood Beam is in place

The view down the Nave in 2007

In 1963 the Revd Sadler wrote about the Town Hill boundary. *"Our Church is strangely situated in some ways; on the side of a hill and only a foot or so from a drop into a road of some ten or more feet. You may have noticed that for some months now the stone wall running as our boundary with the road of Town Hill has, between existing buttresses, an ominous bulge. We feel strongly that this state of affairs might, if left, result in an inconvenient and dangerous breach and form an obstruction on a public highway. Something, therefore, has been determined upon in the way of precaution and prevention. Works in connection with this boundary wall have been ordered and should be in hand sometime this month. All this necessary work will cost money. So that we might not have to spend more than we must, does any reader know of any idle semi-dressed stone (for facing the repaired wall)? From some old or dilapidated cottage, or mine engine-house or the like? IF SO, please contact at once either the Parish Priest or one of the Church Wardens and we will take steps to acquire the stone on reasonable terms… the most reasonable being the form of a pious benefaction! Please keep open eyes and ears."* (Church Magazine)

In 1963 a faculty was issued for: i) re-wiring the Church and ii) for panelling in memory of the Revd G H Barnicoat. (List of Faculties)

The Church was included in the list of buildings of special architectural or historic interest by the Minister of Housing and Local Government on the 30th of May 1967. (Document lodged with the County Records Office)

In 1968 a faculty was issued to grant a licence to the Cornwall County Council for the use of a portion of the churchyard for the purpose of improving the public highway. (List of Faculties)

In 1969 the Church roof was in a bit of a state and work was urgently needed. The Church Magazine stated that an estimate of £520 had been accepted and work would begin shortly. The Vicar explained that the cost would be met from the *"Splendid result of the Annual Sale"* and from monies in hand. This would put a strain on finances and he hoped that the imminent demise of the half-crown would not mean a reduction in collection receipts by the convenience of giving 10 new pence in its stead.

In 1971 the Revd Sadler wrote, *"Any minute now (I hope), men will appear to examine and put to rights the weather vane that crowns the Church steeple. At present it seems to be suffering from partial vertigo!"*

In the same Church Magazine a story concealed a tale of near disaster. It has never been told before, well, not without some form of liquid refreshment! *"At long last and with the co-operation of both the Cornwall County Council and the free labour of the local Round Table, the trees and branches that appeared either dead or dangerous in the Old Burial Ground (euphemistically and unofficially known as the 'Garden of Rest') have been cut down and logged and disposed of at the discretion of the Tablers…to whom we are most grateful for their spirit of community service that led them to this good work for us all."*

What these words of thanks did not reveal is that raw enthusiasm is no substitute for experience and, as one of the merry men who undertook this task, I (Tony Mansell) can say that part way into the operation we had two reasons to rue our rash offer of help. The first involved the near loss of one of our number who, but for a brief moment of rest in his use of a chainsaw, would have been standing directly under a falling trunk. The other involved one of the highest trees which decided to fall in directly the opposite direction to the way which we had planned. Luckily, before it had moved too far, it snagged amongst the adjoining trees giving us time to ponder how much of the Chapel it would actually demolish. Insurance? What insurance? With great presence of mind one of the farmers amongst us attached his tractor to the bottom of the tree and pulled. It worked and, with the centre of gravity transferred, it began its inevitable fall in the correct direction and away from the Chapel. *"Not sure what you were worried about,"* he said as the rest of us quickly collected our things and headed for home.

In 1976 an Archdeacon's Certificate was issued for the replacement of Church windows. (List of Faculties)

In 1978 a faculty was issued to provide: I) new toilet facilities comprising WC and wash hand basin at the rear of the choir vestry and ii) a new oil-fired boiler to replace the old and unusable one. (List of Faculties)

In 1979 a faculty was issued for pews to replace chairs. (List of Faculties)

In 1980 a faculty was issued for: i) the erection of an outdoor crucifix near the south door and ii) the lowering of the west wall of the old burial ground. (List of Faculties)

Do you remember the Argus newspaper? Well, in 1981 it reported that 100 years earlier the Church organ had cost £210 and posed the question of what the current cost would be.

In 1981 a faculty was issued for the installation of a statue of St Agnes. (List of Faculties)

The bookcases at the rear of the Church were donated in memory of Ken Winsor. The commemorative plate states, *"Loyal Member of St Agnes Parish Church 1921-1983"*.

In March 1988 there was concern about the upkeep of the Churchyard and this item appeared in the Parish Magazine. *"During the summer of last year the Manpower Services Commission was asked if labour could be provided for work in the Churchyard: eg the boundary wall needed repointing and capping, paths remaking, steps constructed to the lower churchyard to make access to the graves easier than at present and the retaining walls at the west end of the church and in Town Hill needed attention.*
*   None of this work could be done without the permission of the Diocesan Authorities and so application was made to the legal department of the Diocesan Registrar about the time of Father Michael's departure for Australia…"*
    It was said that the work was undertaken at minimal cost to the Church and the result was of considerable benefit to all.

Writing in the Church Magazine in November 1988 John Briney, the Treasurer, outlined the need for new lighting for the Church. He said that the existing lighting was poor resulting in areas left in shadow. He was also concerned that the addition of various electrical sockets would overload the system and cause a fire. He said, *"Some idea of the age of the system can be judged from the old brown switches and 5-amp plugs"*.
    Competitive quotations were obtained and the South Western Electricity Board undertook the work at a cost of nearly £6,000.

Towards the end of 1988 the Revd Adams decided to discontinue using the granite High Altar in favour of a table. This was very quickly replaced by the Blessed Sacrament Altar – the oak table which had once been the High Altar. During the interregnum period it was all-change as the oak table was returned to the south aisle and the granite High Altar brought back into use.

The 150th anniversary of the third Church was celebrated in May 2001 with an exhibition of old documents relating to the history of the building. Included was the actual consent to demolish the old Church and replace it with a new structure.
    The West Briton reported, *"With the actual public notice calling a meeting to look at tenders for the new Church is an oil painting of the previous Church by Edward Opie, it included the roof of the former market house demolished in 1894.*
    Old photographs of church activities and the centenary celebrations, arranged by Clive Benney, included some of damage to the spire struck by lightning in 1905. A newspaper report says the

shock was felt throughout the district. Lightning played with dazzling brilliancy on the steel cable in Wheal Kitty shaft and miners underground were knocked flat.

The Church was open all weekend and featured flower displays by local groups and a display of Church vestments."

In 2004 the granite High Altar was re-located away from the east wall to allow the Vicar to stand behind it and face the congregation. Malcolm Carveth undertook the task and made light work of what must have been a difficult job.

In September 2006 the West Briton reported that the generosity of St Agnes residents had boosted the repairs fund for the Parish Church. A gift day had produced donations of more than £6,000 towards the £45,000 project.

The newspaper said, "People visiting the area will have noticed that considerable activity has been taking place at the Church recently. Work has begun to replace the lead and tiles on the roof and two cast iron windows in the vestry are to be replaced.

Vicar Alan Bashforth said he was humbled by the response. 'We took over £5,000 on the day and it was all gift aided so it will be around £6,200...At the very least the building will be watertight but it may mean we have funds to do additional work...Our building is still well used and I believe much loved by the community it serves.'"

The Vicarage

Thomas Tonkin wrote that permission to build the 1484 Church was based on certain conditions, one of which was, *"That they should build a convenient house, or chamber, for the use of the Chaplain, who is to celebrate in the Chappel of St Agnes; and is that house which, with the garden, adjoining to Penwennacke (out of the which Barton it was taken), is now called the Vicaridge."*

Betty Tredinnick wrote about it in the St Agnes Museum Trust Journal when she described village life up to about 1840. *"Vicarage (Road) was so called as the Vicar lived in a house on the corner of Vicarage Road and Penwinnick Road where Dale's Garage was later built".*

The vicarage in Trevaunance Road does not appear on the 1838 map and we feel that it is likely that it was built shortly after the Church. It is probable that James Piers St Aubyn, the architect for the Church, also designed the vicarage.

It still looks a fine building and the new Vicar must have been delighted with the capacious home and garden.

The Revd Rudall at the door of the Vicarage in Trevaunance Road sometime around 1914

Writing in the Church Magazine in 1965 the Vicar said, *"The extensive works at the vicarage still go on and we are perforce more or less camping out in it. This is, of course, both avoidable and frustrating but we hope to have an improved dwelling for our successors as well as for ourselves when the plumbers, painters, chippies, electricians and so forth depart. All improvements to and modifications of parsonages make Benefices less domestically unbeneficial and so easier to fill; thus all the upheaval may be a benefaction to posterity in the long view, as well as to the present occupiers in the short. We have hopes of being back to the (improved) normal by the end of this month."*

In 2000 a proposal to sell the vicarage brought forward strong objections from the St Agnes Parish Church Council.

"Dear Mr Laite,
Re: Replacement of the Vicarage at St Agnes
St Agnes is the second largest parish in Cornwall and is made up of a village settlement, two or three hamlets and many widespread rural farms, smallholdings and cottages. It lies half way along the north coast, has three beaches and therefore the main industry is tourism.

The village has a fairly level main street but other streets and roads tend to be very hilly; anywhere outside a half mile limit makes it difficult to walk to the village (Church).

These are our objections to the replacement of our present vicarage:

- *The close proximity of the vicarage to the Church, Church Hall and centre of the village.*
- *A level site making it easily accessible for the disabled – we have several parishioners in wheelchairs.*
- *Easy access for church – the vicar should have easy access to the church and be readily available.*
- *The need to have a large meeting room and church office especially as we are now a united benefice.*
- *The present vicarage is a valuable asset which will not depreciate over the years as a modern house would. The running costs and repairs are comparable with other houses.*
- *The garden is ideal and suitable for church functions.*
- *It is easily identifiable and readily available for people seeking help.*
- *It can accommodate any size family.*
- *The parking provided by the present vicarage is an asset which we would be unable to replace. There is no public parking within a quarter of a mile and in summer (the village) is full and we have double yellow lines throughout. We have a lot of parishioners from outside the immediate area who have no option but to use a car as we have no adequate bus service on Sundays.*
- *We know of several ministers who have said they would have no hesitation in living there.*

We have been able to study the requirements set out in the parsonage design guide and we think our present vicarage answers all the requirements. We do feel our whole village life has been enhanced by the fellowship that has been enjoyed because of the availability of this venue."

The letter was signed by B Thomas and M Whitworth, Church Wardens, on behalf of the parishioners of St Agnes but despite the protest the sale went ahead and the vicarage relocated to Penwinnick Parc.

The Church Hall

The foundation stone of the St Agnes Sunday School Church Hall was laid on the 30th March 1885: a ceremony witnessed by local children who were allowed out of school early. (St Agnes 1001-1999)

The Trust Deed for the building is dated the 6th of August 1884 and states that the building is, *"To be used for religious instruction but not for secular instruction"*. This clearly changed over the years as Maurice Bizley wrote, *"The social life, too, is not neglected for nearby is a large Church Hall, erected in 1885, in which much communal activity takes place"*.

  The hall has seen many changes and, perhaps because of its location, it is still the nearest thing the village has to a village hall.

St Agnes Silver Band used the hall as its practice room for a while as in St Agnes and its Band it says, *"1922 – Band relocates from Peterville to Church Hall"*. In the same book it says, *"In 1922 the band transferred their rehearsal sessions to the Church Hall, an arrangement which continued until 1939"*.

In 1929 the Church Magazine included an item describing the work to the Church Hall.
 "It seems opportune at the moment, to draw your attention to the improvements that have been carried out in the Church Hall.

  The Committee decided at the last meeting that to make the Hall more comfortable and attractive, certain alterations had to be carried out. The electric light has been installed and a ladies dressing room made, using the existing porch for that purpose. The entrance for ladies will now be through the dressing room and men will enter by the west end door.

  The fireplaces have been put in order, the stage lowered and enlarged by means of a drop extension.

  A cloakroom for men at the west end has still to be added, also the pathway widened.

  Needless to say, these alterations will cost money and will lessen the amount we have in hand. It is hoped in the near future to get chairs for seating accommodation in place of the not very comfortable forms which are at present in use. The Treasurer will be grateful for any donation large or small."

In May 1937 St Agnes joined in the celebrations for the Coronation of King George VI and Queen Elizabeth. Frank Carpenter referred to the occasion in his book, St Agnes 1001-1999 and describes the procession which was, *"Led by the St Agnes Town Silver Band to Goonown Playing Field where the Children's Sports were held"*. The day was rounded off with a dance in the Church Hall to the music of the Versatile Dance Band.

On the 17th July 1940 the Royal Cornwall Gazette reported, *"A YMCA centre had been opened in St Agnes Church Hall where meals were served and facilities such as recreation and reading were provided. Mr W W Champness was the leader in charge"*.

In 1945 the Church Magazine referred to the use of the Church Hall for the period of the Second World War. *"During the past six years the Church Hall has been put to very good use by the YMCA which has been very efficiently run, first by Mr Champness and then by Mrs Hancock. Mrs Hancock has been like a mother to many lonely men passing through St Agnes and has tried to bring a touch of home into their lives, which has been much appreciated by them. We have missed our Hall but have been grateful for the good use to which it has been put."*

In 1952 the Hall was used for a BBC recording, for the programme Town Magazine. A letter to St Agnes Band said, *"On June 4th in the Church Hall we are making a recording for subsequent broadcast in which six St Agnes people are going to talk, with a Chairman, about their town, its history, its present life, and their own associations with it".* The Band was asked to provide a piece of music for the programme. It explained that the recording of the band would be, *"As soon after five o'clock as you can get the lads together".* The programme was transmitted on the West of England Home Service on Monday, 28th July 1952 at 7.00pm and for their three minute slot the band were paid the sum £7.7s.0d.

In St Agnes and its Band it says, *"1955 - The Revd G H Barnicoat banned Sunday night concerts in the Church Hall because he considered they were preventing people from attending Church".*

The BBC programme Have A Go with Wilfred Pickles came to St Agnes during the 1950s when St Agnes Silver Band was featured playing the march The Old Bill.
"During the 1960s, folk evenings were very popular and this became a regular feature for a few years. The Church Hall received a makeover to create the atmosphere and without a thought for health &

A Nativity play on the old stage during the mid 1950s (photo by Ken Young)

safety, bales of straw were brought in for seating and candles were distributed around the room. I don't remember anyone even mentioning the fire risk and, thankfully, nothing went wrong. A number of folk singers from around the county took part." (St Agnes and its Band)

In 1963 the Vicar wrote in the Church Magazine, *"If you have not been in the Church Hall lately a great surprise awaits you…and I guarantee, a pleasant surprise. Owing to the drive and generosity of Mrs Olds in giving the materials it has been wholly and tastefully redecorated inside…and not before time! We had by us certain monies which have helped pay for the labour and we also had fitted four electric overhead heaters…two of which were also Mrs Old's gift. For the others we have to pay and you will hear of this from me ere long. This, we hope will do away for good with the coal fires and the ravishes of certain winds which used to envelop us in smoke. So, when I ask for some money for the heaters, give your bit in gratitude for a brighter, cleaner hall. (Next the exterior painting, eh?)"*

The Board of Finance of the Diocese of Truro (Diocesan Authority) became the Church Hall custodian trustee in 1966.

In 1966 it was a slightly different message from the Revd Sadler. *"I must tell you that there is just appearing over the horizon one more financial test: the Church Hall. Most of you will already know that we have had enquiries about our selling it. This entailed delving into the past to discover under whose control it was, interviews with the Lord Bishop and the Archdeacon and the Registrar and a professional valuation. The upshot is that the idea of selling it has been abandoned and the PCC has appointed a sub-committee with power to act. The Hall however, is still in danger of being a bit of a white elephant and we must address ourselves seriously to rehabilitate it forthwith…*

This body consists of Mr F Olds (Chairman), Mr R Hassall (Secretary for all bookings), Mr K Leadbeater (Treasurer) and Mr A Thomas."

The Vicar referred to the many objections to the suggested sale but said that the decision to retain it necessitated urgent action to improve its condition. (St Agnes Church Magazine)

The Vicar continued the story in a later magazine, *"Now is the time to face what it will cost to have a Hall in good repair both without and within. At a conservative estimate this will cost several hundred pounds – the greater part of which must be layed out on urgent work on the exterior of the building…at present one can lift out many of the roof slates – the zinc nails have all perished and who can remember when the place was last painted?"*

The story rumbled on for some time and it is good to read, in 1967, *"The roof is now repaired, the gutters and down-pipes repaired or replaced and the exterior painting now well on the way to completion".* But with that achieved that the horizons were then raised. *"The chief item remaining is to erect a suitable covered porch at the back of the building to make a covered entrance and for use as a secure water-proof storage place for trestles, table tops etc. This will be an expensive item but with the big potential that a sound and well equipped Hall will have…I am aware that an appeal for lots of money for so 'unromantic' a thing as a church hall does not fire people to heroic sacrifice…I have agreed a GIFT DAY…and shall sit-out at the Lych Gate…to receive contributions…I invite you to call upon me that day with the 'necessary'."*

In 1969 the idea of selling the Hall was still on the agenda and it seems that the Parish Council was the interested party. The Vicar seemed keen on the idea and saw it as a way of retaining the Hall for community use. But it did not happen and in 1975 the Vicar wrote in the Church Magazine about the need to replace the roof which would cost about £2,000. He said, *"We realise also that certain basic facilities are either lacking or are in poor condition – the toilets spring to mind".* He referred to a recent meeting of organisations which used the Hall and invited Church members to attend the next one. He finished by saying, *"You will be there, won't you?"*

The next report in the Magazine states, *"The Parochial Church Council accepted…a tender for over £2,000 for the complete renewal of the roof…after hearing of the whole-hearted support…of the congregation…and after the assurance of help from some of the organisations and societies who use the Hall.*

Mr Donald Blight has been invited by the Council to take steps for the raising of the money…"

Under the heading of *"Never a dull moment"* the Church Warden related the story of receiving unexpected guests for supper on the rainy night of the 16th August 1977. *"The visitors were 12 (rather large) German Scouts who needed shelter for the night. The Church Hall being in use until 10.30pm we, of course, invited them in. Little did we think that at 11.30pm we should be eating their noodles and mince mixed with at least three bottles of ketchup (cooked by themselves in an enormous pan, with Diana's help and lots of laughter). After this and two rounds of tea – 16 cups each time – we listened and joined in with their songs accompanied by guitars. They finally left at 12.20pm to go to the Church Hall. They were very grateful, thoroughly enjoyed their visit to St Agnes and we are expecting some letters when they return to Germany."*

In 1982 the call went out for pre-payment electricity meters, electric boilers for tea-making, electric cookers, kitchen tables and white cups and saucers. Information was to be passed to Mr Blight or Mrs Tonkin who said, *"The Church Hall equipment is getting old even faster than we are!"*
(Church Magazine April 1982)

The condition of the Hall was the cause of some concern again in 1993 when a report in the Church Magazine raised the question *"What's happening to the Church Hall?"* It talked of the future of the Church Hall being shrouded in uncertainty and said it was clear to everyone, including the Fire Prevention Officer, that some restoration and renovation work was necessary to bring the building up to standard.

The reason for the word *"uncertainty"* then became apparent as it stated, *"At the same time as the PCC was considering schemes for upgrading the building it became apparent that the County Library Service was looking for new premises. It had long been felt by some that a hall within the curtilage of the churchyard would have many benefits, not least that it would remove the dangerous and time-consuming 'crocodiling' of children between Hall and Church through a busy narrow street, the paving of which is so narrow as to be made impassable by the wing mirrors of parked cars.*

The Church Hall building was offered to the Library Service in the hope that its sale would enable a modern, purpose-built unit to be erected adjacent to the Church. Although the County Council were quite enthusiastic at the possibility of moving its Library into the centre of the village, the alternative scheme of constructing a new library building on the Carrick District Council owned site adjacent to the present portable unit proved to be the more economic solution."

The report goes on to outline the task of upgrading the Hall to make it suitable for use by the community. The idea of leasing the building to a *"Village Hall Committee,"* had been considered but rejected.

It continued, *"Even the minimum of works to comply with the requirements of the statutory authorities and to make the building safe and comfortable will probably cost nearly £10,000 so a lot of hard work lies before us. There was an outcry from some sectors of the community when it was feared that the facilities of the Church Hall would no longer be available. We trust that their enthusiasm for the retention of the Hall will be matched by the generosity of their support for its Restoration Fund."*

Vicars & Curates

We have not included a list of Vicars and Curates prior to 1846, the point at which St Agnes became an independent ecclesiastical Church. However, a very full and interesting list can be found in the book Friendly Retreat.

Vicars of St Agnes Parish Church as shown on the plaque on the west wall

1846 - 1875	Revd A A Vawdrey
1875 - 1886	Revd E L Salisbury
1887 - 1922	Revd A Rudall
1923 - 1933	Revd W H Browne
1933 - 1937	Revd C G Roffe-Silvester
1937 - 1958	Revd G H Barnicoat
1959 - 1972	Revd F A Sadler
1973 - 1987	Revd A M Williamson
1988 - 1999	Revd M J Adams
2001 -	Revd A G Bashforth

The Revd Michael Adams was also the Priest in charge at Mithian and Mount Hawke Churches and in 2001 the three benefices were formally united.

Assistant Curates of St Agnes Parish Church

1865	Revd C T Knapp
1882	Revd Pender Hodge Cudlip
1891	Revd Thomas Bennetts
1898	Revd Philip Morgan
1904	Revd Joseph Rawson
1909	Revd Sidney John Richards
1912	Revd Philip Morgan (Returned to the post)
1914	Revd Rupert Henry Jones
1915 - 1920	Revd Barry
1922	Revd W D Hawken (Priest in charge for a short while)
1925 - 1931	Revd C V Lawson
1925 - 1927	Revd E Faull
1931	Revd Clement William Cockerell
1934	Revd Arthur Cornelius Hosken
1937 - 1948	Canon Frederick Robert Carr
1948 - 2003	We believe that the role was discontinued during this period
2003 - 2006	Revd Hilary Sampson

We are indebted to the late Maurice Bizley for some of the information in this section.

Bell Ringing

In 1905 lightning struck the Church and, perhaps seizing the opportunity, it was decided to undertake the refurbishment of the bells. The Royal Cornwall Gazette stated, *"The bells were sent forward to Messrs Taylor's bell foundry at Loughborough. The tenor bell was dated 1748 but the others were cast 100 years later,"* and John King wrote, *"The bells were recast in 1905 as a memorial to Alderman William Lawrence by his son Sir Edwin Durning Lawrence".*

In August of that year a fete and bazaar was held in Dr Whitworth's grounds to raise money towards the cost of re-hanging and on the 23rd of November 1905 the Royal Cornwall Gazette reported, *"Work to re-hang the bells started on Monday – scaffolding around the tower and steeple was removed and the Church has thus regained its normal appearance. The dedication will take place on the 1st of December."* (RCG 23rd November 1905) John Taylor & Co undertook the work, re-hanging the bells in a new iron frame.

The completion of the work was well celebrated as shown by this report. *"The pretty little Church of St Agnes was well filled on Friday afternoon, on the occasion of the dedication of the Church bells which have recently been re-cast and rehung. The cost of re-hanging the bells and building the steeple was £150 which is being met by the parishioners themselves. About £120 has already been raised. Sir Edward Durning-Lawrence has very kindly consented to defray the cost of recasting the bells, this coming to about £70.*

The Bishop, accompanied by the choir and clergy, went to the belfry and said the dedicatory prayer, after which the St Agnes band of ringers rang a short peal, their light and sweet tone being the subject of admiration and pleasure. The ringers were: Treble - Wm Vanstone, 2nd – H Pearse, 3rd – Thomas J Tresize, 4th – W Hodge, 5th – J H Quick and tenor – F O Rillstone." (The West Briton 8th December 1905)

The bell ringers' outing is a regular feature of Church life and on the 20th September 1921 the Royal Cornwall Gazette reported, *"The ringers of St Agnes Parish Church restored to Plymouth on Saturday for their outing. A stay of nearly 12 hours enabled them to have an enjoyable day."*

The Church Magazine in 1929 included the following notice: *"A meeting of the ringers was held in the vestry on Tuesday March 19th at 8.00pm. The following is a full list of ringers – A Harris (Captain), R J Dibbs (Vice-Captain), V Whitta, A Chamberlain, J Clissold, C V Lawson, W Tredinnick, F Tredinnick, J Stanaway and W Waters. Those who did not attend the meeting or send any reason for their absence have been crossed off the list."*

In 1934 the Magazine reported, *"For this ensuing year the Captain and Vice-Captain have changed places, Mr Dibbs becoming Captain and Mr Harris Vice-Captain. I always feel that we should be grateful to our bell ringers, especially to so keen a team as we have in this Parish. There have been some new members of the Guild during the past year and when they have become more experienced we hope it may be possible to arrange for them to take part in some of the ringing festivals that are held at different churches in the Diocese. One thing that is needed is a set of hand bells. A good major set would cost £8. 10s .0d, though a smaller set could be bought for £7. 0s. 0d. A contribution has already been promised towards this and I should be grateful for some further contributions from members of the congregation who appreciate our Church bells and the good services of those who ring them."*

The Vicar presided over the annual meeting in 1935 when Mr Dibbs was re-elected as Captain and Mr F Tredinnick elected as Vice-Captain. Mr J Stanaway was re-elected as Steeple-keeper and was thanked for the work that he had done.

The Church Magazine recorded that J Taylor & Co had estimated the cost of re-conditioning the bells as £83 and this had been placed before the Parochial Church Council but that they had deferred the matter for the time. The report continued, *"To enable better progress to be made in method-ringing a set of hand bells is needed and much disappointment was felt that there had been absolutely no response to the appeal which the Vicar had made in the Parish Magazine last year for help towards buying a set of hand bells…"*

In 1936 the Vicar, Revd Roffe-Silvester, voiced his concern at the lack of interest taken in the Church bells and penned the following authoritative history of bells and bell ringing.

"I sometimes wonder how much interest is taken in our Church bells. About two years ago I appealed twice over in this Magazine for contributions towards purchasing a set of hand bells for our ringers in order that they might be able to practise more easily but I did not receive a single offer. And, as the members of the Parochial Church Council know, it may be necessary to spend rather a large sum of money on re-conditioning the bells in our Church tower in the not very far distant future.

Of all Church fittings bells have the misfortune to be the most neglected by the general public. Their sound is familiar, they presence is taken for granted but the bells themselves are practically unknown by reason of their position. Yet Church bells are full of the deepest interest.

The origin of bells lies in the distant centuries long before the Christian era and probably began with the cymbal and the gong. We know that bells of an immense size were cast in China and the East several centuries before Christ. And small bells are mentioned in the Bible in the book of Exodus.

Bells for calling worshippers to Church were at first quite small and were held in the hand; they were not cast by a bell-founder but were made of sheets of metal riveted together like the modern cow-bell…The first record of an English bell-founder casting a bell dates from the tenth century… Church bells have always been regarded as holy and sacred and are always carefully and solemnly blessed and in the prayers of their dedication there is a petition that the sound of the bell may avail to summon the faithful and excite their devotion…

The quality of a bell depends on a number of factors; the proportions of copper and tin in the alloy must be correct as also must be the shape and proportions of the bell itself. And it is interesting to note that the modern bells of today are being made longer and more after the mediaeval style than those of the last three centuries.

In recent years great improvements have been made in the tuning. I wonder whether you have noticed that a bell does not give forth one single note like the wire of a piano but a whole series of notes; therefore a bell has not only to be tuned with the others in its particular ring but also tuned with itself. Modern methods employed during the last forty years have made tuning an exact science whereas previously it had been, to some extent, a matter of luck. And one is glad to know that the English bell-founders are absolutely unsurpassed anywhere in the world.

Of great bells the largest in the world, so far as is known, is the big bell in Moscow known as 'the King of Bells' or 'Big John'; this was cast in the 18th century and weighs about 200 tons though it is possible that even this is exceeded by some of the bells in China and Burma of which we have no authentic records of their weights.

Moscow possesses two others of the same period weighing respectively 171 tons and 110 tons. But it must be remembered however, that these bells are intended to be stationary or 'dead'. The largest bell in England is 'Great Paul' which, though a midget in comparison with the Russian bells, weighs sixteen and three-quarter tons and is swung. Our second in size, 'Big Ben,' of Westminster, weighs thirteen and a half tons; while other large bells of about ten tons exist at York, Manchester, Beverley and other places.

The heaviest bell to be actually rung in a peal is the tenor of the twelve bells at Exeter (72 cwt) and the second is that at St Paul's (62 cwt); both these have been rung single-handed in peals lasting four hours. It is interesting to compare these tremendous bells with our own at St Agnes of which the tenor (the heaviest) weighs but 7 cwt.

The English have always liked to swing their bells; therefore the bells were fitted with wheels so that the ropes could be taken down vertically into a ringing chamber to make the task easier and avoid undue wear. They were at first fitted with quarter and half wheels; but in the early 17th century an improvement was introduced in the complete wheel, which made it possible to ring the bell right up through a full circle into the inverted position. And it is to this that we owe the full science of what is called, 'change-ringing' as it is today. Before this invention each bell had swung in its own time as a pendulum, making possible only a discordant jangling or at very best the repetitions of a fixed order, as in chiming but now it became possible for the ringer, by holding his bell poised at the point of balance, to control the timing himself and thus perform the variations of order known as 'changes'.

England is the only country in Europe where the science and method of 'change-ringing' is practised. On the continent the bells are not rung in any particular order but anyhow, with a confused jangling.

In England the 17th century saw the beginning of change-ringing, from modest beginnings to its present form in which all the bells constantly move to and fro in a definite order, changing their sequence at each stroke according to recognised methods.

For the sake of those who may know but little about the mysteries of change-ringing I will explain that the bells are referred to by numbers, from the smallest, number 1, known as the 'treble', to the largest, known as the 'tenor'. When rung down the scale from treble to tenor they are said to be rung in 'rounds' and variations of this order are termed 'changes'.

A 'peal' is a length of 5,000 changes or more, while anything shorter is a 'touch'. All peals and touches begin and end with rounds and must be 'true,' that is they must not contain any particular change more than once."

The complete article is rather lengthy and becomes increasingly detailed and complicated but for the aficionado it will be of interest and reference to the full text in the Church Magazine may prove rewarding.

At the Annual Meeting of the bell ringers in 1948 Mr A Harris was re-elected as Captain of the Tower and Mr W M Harper as Vice-Captain. The Church Magazine reported, *"The Vicar thanked them for the important piece of work that they did. For good ringing practice was necessary. Before the War the ringers met twice a week for practice but it is now only possible to meet for an hour and a half on Tuesday evenings. It is important that every ringer should come to this.*

A delightful outing was held on Whit Monday in perfect weather. Towers at Probus, St Austell, Lanhydrock, Bodmin and Roche were visited. The party stopped for lunch at Carlyon Bay and were entertained at Lanhydrock by Viscount Cliffden. Our ringers were congratulated at several Towers on their performance. And they can sing too; but perhaps this was due to the quantity of tea consumed."

In the 1951 book about the Church, Maurice and Alice Bizley suggest that the six bells were transferred from the old to the new Church but they also say that four of them bore the inscription *"C & G Mears, Founders, London, 1850"*. It would seem that two were actually transferred as these were inscribed with the words, *"Thos Lester of London made us all, 1748"*. The other four were purchased for the new building and as Mears bought the bell foundry of Thos Lester during the late 1700s, it seems likely that all of the bells were made at the same location.

Mr N T Smith took over as Captain in 1956 and Miss Ackroyd was elected Vice-Captain. A tribute was paid to the late Captain, Mr A Harris, for all he had done in the interest of ringing.

An account of the 1956 bell ringers outing was written by one of the party and included in the Church Magazine. *"The bell ringers held their annual outing on Whit Monday. We left the Church at 9.00am after a short service. It was a mystery tour arranged by our Captain Mr Smith and Miss Ackroyd. We had beautiful weather and everyone enjoyed themselves. We rang at five churches, St Erme, St Enoder, Roche, Lanhydrock and Egloshayle. We spent the afternoon looking around Viscount Clifden's estate. The gardens and flowers were really lovely. In the evening we came back to Newquay and spent an hour there. By that time most of us were tired so we arrived home about 10.00pm. We offer our thanks to those who arranged the trip and to Mr Robin Kellow for driving the bus."*

In 1957 the Church Magazine described the bell ringers' outing. *"As regards the weather, the bell ringers had far more than they expected, but certainly deserved, for their outing. After the damping we had on Whitsunday we contemplated the weather with trepidation but awoke to find the sun shining and it turned out a glorious day. And we had a wonderful time too. This year, members of the Tower of St Erme joined forces with us, so after a short service in Church, we went to Truro to pick them up. From there we went to Lelant for the first peal and then on to Zennor. The bells here were on the heavy side but our ringers got on very well. We went on to Lands End for lunch and it was delightful sitting in the sun at the extreme tip of England looking out over the sea. With Longships Lighthouse to the left and the Scilly Isles to the right, one could picture shipwrecks and smuggling in the days gone by. After lunch the party stopped for a peal at Sennen, where the bells were light. From there we made towards Penzance, turning off to visit the Tower of Paul. All considered that the bells here were excellent and they had some of the best peals of the day. Then on to Penzance where we stopped for over an hour for tea and bacon and eggs and such like things were very welcome, not to mention numerous cups of tea. The last peal was at Madron and sometime was spent here. So home, with a stop at Hayle for chips, reaching St Agnes at 10 o'clock after a thirteen hour outing. We were all grateful to our Captain Mr Tre Smith for the splendid day he had arranged; and to the Captain of St Erme Tower who was in charge of the change ringing. He ought to know something about it having been a ringer for fifty years."*

In 1958 the annual outing took the ringers to St Teath, Week St Mary, Bude for lunch, Launceston, Altarnun – the Cathedral of the Moor – to Jamaica Inn for pasties and to Bodmin for fish and chips. They arrived back at St Agnes at 11.00pm tired and happy (and full I should think!) The Captain, Tre Smith, and Vice-Captain, Mr Hockaday, were thanked for organising the day.

In 1962 the bell ringers of St Agnes became affiliated to the Truro Diocesan Guild of Ringers and took part in a campanological contest at St Mewan where they emerged with two certificates of merit. The report concludes that they had, *"A whale of a tea!"*

At the AGM in 1963 George Repper and Fred Olds were re-elected as Captain and Vice-Captain. The Vicar commented that there were less Sundays with no peals and there was *"...a noticeable increase in change-ringing".*

Lady bell ringers – circa 1965
Maureen Blight, Margaret Harper, Mrs Todd (at back), Pam Ely, unknown and Eleanor Smith

In 1965 the ringers returned home from the St Erme Festival with two 1st class certificates for Round and Change Test Ringing. The Vicar said, *"I hope I have the technicalities accurate! This is a credit to the Church and must be a fine encouragement to the ringers of whom we are proud."*

I (Tony Mansell) played in St Agnes Silver Band for many years and recall that one of our rehearsal nights coincided with bell ringing practice. The bandroom is next to the Church and only a short while after we'd started playing, our concentration would be shattered. Brass against bronze - who would win? We didn't really stand a chance. I don't think that any of us understand the subtleties of campanology nor why it was necessary to rehearse taking turns to pull a piece of rope.

Now I've managed to upset all the bell ringers but in my defence I will say that it was a long time ago and it really did cause us some grief.

This article on the bells at St Agnes was included in one of the 1971 Church Magazines.
"So let's start at the west end of the Church with the bells. There are six of these – two made (or 'cast' as they say of bells) as long ago as 1748 and four in 1850. Their main use is to give notice of some act or other of Public Worship which is shortly to be offered to God's Majesty and to summon His people to come and take part in that worship. They also tell of the joy of weddings and (only one of them) of the solemn times of funerals. At present we have enthusiastic ringers and the bells are rung regularly and well and I am sure that if any of you who read this would care to have a go at ringing, you will be welcomed if you tell the Captain of the Tower, Mr George Repper. There have been several recruits of late to the art of campanology (the posh name for bell ringing). In too many churches the art and honour of bell ringing is marred by the fact that people will come regularly enough to ring the bells (for, I believe, it is a fascinating art) and then go off before the worship to which those very bells are a summons! This is NOT the way with St Agnes ringers I am happy to say.
Did you know that during the last Great War – 1939/45 – the Government decreed that no church bells were to be rung at all unless as a signal that this country was being invaded by its enemies. Imagine then, the special joy when that ban was lifted and the bells might once again be used for their proper purpose. Indeed, when you hear them ringing it would be good that you breathe a Thank You to God for preserving your parents and elders from the horrors of invasion and occupation by a ruthless enemy – a fate endured by so many other countries in Europe. So dear children, be proud of our bells and see to it that they never cease to summon us all to adore Him whose mercy endureth for ever."

In 1974 the Vicar referred to the work being carried out to replace the bearings on the bells. *"We have heard from the firm who is going to rehang our bells. They plan to start work on Monday the 6th May so presumably from that date our bells will be silent. How long they will be out of action we do not know but we hope that it is not too many weeks."*

In 1975 he wrote of his concern at the delay in carrying out work to the bells. *"It is exactly twelve months ago that I wrote in the Magazine that the firm Taylors of Loughborough would be starting work on re-hanging our bells in May 1974. I expressed the hope that the bells would not be silent for too many weeks. Now, exactly fifty-two weeks later, the bell hangers will be returning to complete the work of fitting new bearings to the bells…"*

Anyone wishing to learn the art of bell ringing was asked to contact either Mr G Repper (Captain) or Mr Tonkin (Vice-Captain).

The rededication of the bells - Miss "Bobby" Martin, Pam Roberts, George Repper, the Revd Michael Williamson, Claude Tonkin, Gillian Tonkin (later Clarke) and Helen Tonkin (later Benney)

In 1976 the ringers left at 9.00am on Mr C Williams' luxury coach and visited Perran-ar-Worthal, Constantine, Mullion for lunch with Cornish pasties, Cury, St Hilary, Penzance for tea and shopping and then to the famous church at Paul. The final stop was to St Ives for more food, the traditional fish and chips.

For some reason there was a late start to the 1977 outing but when they eventually got under way they headed for their first stop, at Callington. Pam Roberts, the Secretary to the bell ringers, wrote. *"We felt refreshed after the break and a cuppa and proceeded on our journey"*. On to Tavistock for lunch and, *"...a wee look around the shops"*. On to the village of Whitchurch and then to Eggbuckland where there was a Jubilee party in progress. By this time they must have been hungry - again - so it was on to Plymouth where they enjoyed another cuppa but were disappointed to find the shops closed. As Pam said, *"Much to the relief of the male members of the party"*. It was then back to Menheniott for fish and chips at Lanivet.

In 1978 Tina Tonkin told the story of the bell ringers outing. *"We left St Agnes at 9.00am on a lovely morning. After picking up some people at Peterville and Goonbell we started on our way for St Keyne Church, our first stop.*

St Keyne Church was a small but very well kept church. The bells were very difficult to ring as the sallys were so high and the tallest of our ringers could not reach them. We rang a short peal and then moved on to our next church, North Petherwin.

69

We were late arriving here as we missed our turning. The Church was beautifully kept and the bells were a pleasure to ring unlike our first stop. We were met by an old gentleman who informed us that when the bells were re-hung the Revd Cradock (former Vicar of Mount Hawke) was Vicar of this Parish. There was an old pair of stocks in the Church and some of the children of our party enjoyed putting one another in them. So we left for Bude where we had dinner.

When we arrived at Poughhill the weather had changed and it began to drizzle. We were met at the door by three of their ringers. We all had an enjoyable ring, including our three learners...our next church was Marhamchurch. The bells were very much like our own...our last Church was at St Teath but we were unable to ring there as the bells were out of action.

We stopped at Lanivet for supper and arrived back in St Agnes at 9.00pm. The day was very enjoyable and although it started to rain after dinner the sun still shone from the hedgerows, from the primroses and other spring flowers."

In 1981 the report of the annual outing talked of the anticipation, *"No one except the committee know where we are going".* It went on to say, *"This year there had been vague rumours that it would be 'up-country'.*

As we turned up the A30 towards Bodmin the rumour seemed to be right. Then, at Chybucca, we turned off towards Truro...Kenwyn first stop." On to St Austell and Lostwithiel where the bells were described as *"very nice"* and the ringing *"excellent".* Lunch at Saltash and a trip, *"Over the new bridge to England".* The foreign exposure was short and there was a quick return to Saltash and on to Botus Fleming, Pillaton and the final stop at St Ive. The report concluded with, *"By now we were used to heavy bells, we had a good ring again, until Mr Howlett narrowly missed hanging himself as we rang down! At least, that was the opinion of our Captain, Mr Repper.*

Problems apart it was a very enjoyable day...We have a very promising band of young ringers. Tina Tonkin, who although young is an 'old hand' really, now very ably calls our changes. Mention should also be made of the hard work put in by Mr Tonkin and Mr Roberts on the heaviest bells."

George Alan Repper died on the 24th of July 1982 – he was 81. An entry in the Church Magazine by St Agnes Church bell ringers said, *"He was Captain of the bell ringers until recently. George, as he was always known, had been a ringer since 1919 and Captain of the Tower since 1961. He was a chorister too for very many years and was a regular, loyal and faithful Church member."*

A screen to the tower was erected to his memory; it has a small plaque which reads, *"In Memory of George Repper bell ringer 1919-1982"*

In 1983 Gordon Roberts was the Captain, Mrs P Roberts the Vice-Captain and Miss S R Martin was Secretary. The Vicar thanked the ringers for their work during the past year and referred to the difficulty in raising a team for Evensong. He added, *"Bell ringing is an art and very interesting. It is not just a matter of 'pulling a rope'. As in any form of art it takes practice to become a skilled ringer and much enjoyment can be had, together with the knowledge that one is giving a service – both to God and to the Church.*

There is a special camaraderie amongst ringers and a visiting ringer will always be made welcome in another tower wherever that may be."

In 1984 Gordon Roberts was re-elected Captain of the Tower, Claude Tonkin became Vice-Captain and Helen Benney the Secretary and Training Officer with special responsibility for teaching young ringers.

In March 1988 it was *"Calling all bell ringers"* with this notice in the Church Magazine.

"At a recent meeting of the St Agnes Ringers it was decided that the bells would be rung regularly for the morning service at 10.00am And what a joy it is to hear them calling the people to worship. The Captain of the Tower appeals to anyone who can ring to come forward for practice on Wednesday evenings...don't be shy, ring now!"

The bell ringers on the 1999 annual outing – Helen Benney (née Tonkin), Claude Tonkin, Kay Adams, Alan Nash, Hazel Spence, Arthur Hicks, Annie Holland and Geoff Holland

On the 15th of March 2001 the West Briton included the following report. *"For the first time in almost 100 years six huge bells have been painstakingly removed from St Agnes Parish Church to be restored. A crowd gathered outside St Agnes Hotel on Friday to witness the rare event as the bells were lowered with ropes from the narrow tower and loaded on to a transporter destined for a specialist firm in Bridport. The bells, which were last refitted into the 400-year old tower in 1905, weigh more than half a tonne.*

Bell ringers Geoff Holland and Alan Nash were given the difficult job of starting to dismantle the rusty framework surrounding the bells. Mr Holland told the West Briton: 'The steel frame had started to rust away and the bells were desperately in need of renovation but it has not been an easy task to dismantle it all. There were six bells in two tiers all fitted together like a jigsaw puzzle which we have had to take apart piece by piece. It has been a mammoth task.'

It has been down to the bell ringers to raise money for the project which could cost up to £20,000 and funds are still being sought. 'We had a generous donation following a bereavement. We have also held various events. When we do weddings we make a charge but whereas ringers at other churches share the proceeds, we have been putting it into a kitty which has all added up.'

71

The bells, made of copper and tin, are to be restored by a firm called Andrew Nicholson. The aim is to have them back in place in the tower in May in time for the Church's 150th anniversary – the Church being newer than the original tower. 'Hopefully they will sound better,' said Mr Holland."

Annie Holland wrote of the, *"Four things which impressed us all. Firstly the ambition and ingenuity with which six bells were hung in such a tiny space, secondly, the engineering feat which kept them there – the middle layer of the frame was jointed; thirdly, the size – they were all much bigger than we had appreciated and lastly, they are really pretty bells. The casting is smooth, they are encircled by a row of flowers cast into the bell metal and the tenor was cast with details of the 18th century ring which were melted down to give us our present six."*

The West Briton of the 31st of May 2001 announced, *"Bells ring out for celebration".* The bells had been silent for six weeks but following their restoration they rang out for the Sunday service and to mark the 150th anniversary of the present Church building. The report said, *"The six bells and tower are from the 15th century second Church on the site. The current Church was built when St Agnes became a parish in its own right and separate from Perranzabuloe…Much of the £14,000 cost of the bell's restoration has been met from a legacy of Mr S Holmes. With fundraising and donations about £500 has still to be found.*

The Church was full on Sunday morning for the rededication of the ringers and bells in a service shared by the Revd Alan Bashforth, the newly installed Vicar, and Canon Anthony Phillips, the Canon Theologian of the Truro Diocese, who also preached.

Local Methodists and Catholics joined the congregation for an evening united service led by Mr Bashforth with address by the Revd Bev Hollings, the Methodist minister."

After giving thanks to many people and organisations the Revd Alan Bashforth said in the order of service, *"Finally, on behalf of the PCC, the people of the Church, and indeed the people of the Village, I would like to thank the ringers themselves, without whose efforts the project would not have happened at all. Their roll of honour, in no particular order, reads like this: Annie Holland, Geoff Holland, Helen Benney, Claude Tonkin, Rosie Falco, Joe Hart, Alan Nash, Hazel Spence & Arthur Hicks. With perhaps special mention to Geoff and Alan whose blood, sweat, toil and tears made a £25,000 project an awful lot cheaper."*

Registers

The Parish Registers date from 1653 and according to Maurice and Alice Bizley the earliest volume has parchment leaves and is bound in leather; some of the pages are stained but the writing is fairly legible.

The entries prior to 1688 have been copied from the *"Ancient Registers since 1653, and carefully placed in this book by me, D E F Gowen"*. It contains baptisms from 1653 to 1718, marriages from 1674 to 1727 and burials from 1674 to 1712 and in the case of baptisms some of the entries are consolidated so that whole families appear one after the other.

An old Church bier now an exhibit at St Agnes Parish Museum

The first marriage reads, "Stephen Polkinhorne was married 20 Jan 1674". Note that his wife's name is not mentioned. The first entry in which both names are recorded is, "Samuel Geare and Susan Harris married 21 May, 1696".

On the 3rd May 1807 John Luke of Perranzabuloe married Jenifer Rogers but the marriage was not legal as their banns had not been published at Perranzabuloe. It required another ceremony - on the 25th May 1807.

Many entries appear with the word *"Sojourner"* next to the name and *"William Harris and Mary Chapple both sojourners, married 3 Nov., 1792"*. (The word *"sojourn"* means temporary stay)

A note in the Perranzabuloe Register indicates an important event for that Parish. *"From 10 May, 1803 to 13 June, 1805, marriages (in Perranzabuloe Parish) were solemnized at St Agnes Church, there being no Church in Peranzabuloe."* This was during the rebuilding of their Parish Church.

It is not unusual to find Biblical names in Parish Registers and St Agnes is no exception. On the 20th October 1799 Mahershalalhashbaz Richards married Emblyn Allen. He must have liked his given name as he also used it for his son.

The first baptism officially recorded in the Register is that of William, son of John Trezise, on the 1st December 1653, but there are seven entries on the fly leaf. The first was, *"Mrs Mary Newgam baptized in the yeare of our Lord 1601"*.

In the Second Register the section devoted to burials is headed, *"A True List of those that have been Buried in ye Pish of St Agnes since the 7th of April, 1726 in Order according to a late Act of Parliament, Intituled an Act for burying in Woollen etc"*.

The Burying in Wool Act of 1666 required the dead to be buried in English woollen shrouds to the exclusion of any foreign textiles. It was required that an affidavit be sworn in front of a Justice of the Peace confirming burial in wool with the punishment of a £5 fee. Parish registers were marked to confirm that an affidavit had been sworn or marked *"naked"* for those too poor to afford the woollen shroud. The law fell into disuse in the late 18th century and was later repealed.

The Register records a marriage on the 1st of April 1788 - that of Thomas Lawrence and Mary Tonkin, a sojourner. Their eldest son, William Lawrence the Elder, was born at St Agnes on the 4th February 1789 and, like his father, he was a carpenter. In 1808, at the age of 19, he left St Agnes with two guineas in his pocket and his bag of tools. With two friends he worked his way to Plymouth where he took a ship for London. By the age of 25 he had set up in business at Hoxton and two years later he opened a premises at Cheapside. He became a leading citizen of the city being elected an Alderman in 1848 and the Sheriff of London in 1849 but he did not forget the village of his birth and was largely instrumental in the provision of new schoolrooms for the British School.

Three of his ten children were knighted and Edwin, the youngest, had a very distinguished career as an industrialist, writer, politician and philanthropist. He was educated at University College London and was a Member of Parliament for Truro. In 1894 he founded the St Agnes and District Nursing Association and endowed it with the income from two cottages and other investments. He was knighted in 1898 and took the name Durning Lawrence.

The oldest surviving St Agnes register was on show at a weekend exhibition in May 2001. In its report the West Briton stated, *"At the time of the new Church many marrying couples and their witnesses could not read or write signing the register with their 'mark,' explained David Thomas, in notes to these County Records Office documents"*.

Stories

The story of St Agnes men trying to hedge in a cuckoo is well told and we have not included it here but the less familiar story of an attempt to increase the height of the Church tower is worth repeating. The story as displayed in the Parish Museum goes something like this.

"As for that theere story they goat 'bout us, that we dunged our tower to make un graw, 'twas nawthin moore than this:

'I'll have ivy graw oal roun' the tower,' says the passon.

'And so you shall, my deer,' says the churchwarden.

And when the passon was gone, he beginned to put some in: a Trura man looked in and seed un, and thot he was dungin' the tower, to maake un graw, and went and said so: and from that time they do ax how the tower do git on. And that's how it was, and nawthin' moore. And the ivy never grawed, nor the tower of coose; and the moore the pity, for he's oncommon short, but we're goin' to have a new waun."

A local story connects St Agnes with the giant – Bolster. John Kinsman, a Mount Hawke man, told it in The Cornish Handbook in 1921; we will let him tell the story.

"The district lying between St Agnes Beacon and the edge of the cliffs was the scene of giant Bolster's exploits, one of the most praiseworthy of which was his fight with Satan, whom he drove out of the district by hurling huge rocks at him across the space between Beacon Hill and Carn Brea. His opponent has never been seen in the district since, and the struggle accounts for the strange fact that, while Carn Brea is covered with huge masses of rocks, the Beacon is quite bare.

Unbelievers may doubt the story; but the rocks are there as witnesses, and in the valley leading to the sea at Chapel Porth there is the impress of Bolster's foot imprinted on the everlasting rock when he stepped down to pursue his adversary."

A story about Polperro tells of a fault in the slate formations which is said to be the spot chosen on one occasion by Satan for his appearance on earth. The Devil's Quoits are alleged to have been used by their namesake and his friends in their games but, says John Kinsman, *"This must have been in the dark days before Giant Bolster fought his great battle and sent Satan in hot haste out of the Duchy, never to return!"*

The other story is not so creditable. Bolster, although a married man, fell in love with St Agnes and pursued her persistently until she had to resort to female guile to avoid him - by pretending to return his affection. Taking him to the cliff a few hundred yards east of Wheal Coates Mine, she pointed to a small hole in the rock and told Bolster that if he would give her proof of his sincerity she would be his. The task she gave him was to fill the hole with his blood as a token of his love. Bolster looked at the opening in the rock and laughed: he would fill it without any difficulty. He opened a vein and the red blood flowed into the hole but it did not fill. St Agnes knew that the small fissure ran through the rock to a cavern at the foot of the cliff and as his blood continued to flow Bolster collapsed and died.
By this act St Agnes was rid of an embarrassing lover.

The Mare's Egg is another interesting local story. It seems that a St Agnes miner saw a man carrying a pumpkin. Never having seen one before he asked what it was and was informed that it was a Mare's Egg which would hatch out a *"pretty little colt"*. The miner bought it and took it home and kept it wrapped up for a year. As instructed, he then rolled the *"egg"* down from the top of the Beacon, expecting a colt to appear. When it was part way down the slope it ran into a furze bush from where a frightened hare shot out. Seeing this the excited miner shouted:

"Loar, what a little beauty tes, a racer sure he'll be
Ef ever I in oal my life such a putty colt did see
But I must run or else I fear he'll run from me away"
So off he set – the sequel we sure have no need to say.

The Vicar must have had a smile on his face as he inserted the following item in the Church Magazine. He said, *"I am indebted to a correspondent for the following: A Local preacher who for years had been a pillar of nonconformity fell into disagreement with the leading lights of the Chapel and, as a result, began to attend Church instead. 'Yes Sir.' He explained to the Vicar, 'after such treatment as they gave I, for the future I chucks all religion and I goes to Church'."*

Another story from the Church Magazine. *"A ten year-old boy told his mother, 'Our teacher told us how God sent Moses behind the enemy lines to rescue the Israelites from the Egyptians. He brought them to the Red Sea and then ordered his engineers to build a pontoon bridge. After they had all passed over, Moses looked up and saw the Egyptian tanks coming. Quick as a flash Moses grabbed his walkie-talkie and ordered his airforce to bomb the bridge to save the Israelites.'*

'David,' exclaimed his mother, 'Is that how your teacher told the story?'

'Well...not exactly,' David admitted, 'but if I told it her way you'd never believe it'."

The true tale of the Revd C G Roffe-Silvester and his menagerie is remembered by a few people and the story of his pet monkey must have caused a few chuckles across the years - at the expense of the unfortunate pet. It seems that it escaped and to avoid recapture it climbed an electricity pole by the bakery. Jack Williams who was a choirboy at the time recalls it vividly but couldn't confirm its sad end which occurred when he tried to swing from the wires. He was electrocuted and his rigid little body had to remain there until arrangements could be made to remove it for burial.

A snow scene of the Church and Stippy Stappy in the 1960s - photo by Ken Young

Acknowledgements

Our thanks go to all those people who have been so generous in giving their time to make this book possible particularly the Revd Alan Bashforth who has spent many hours pouring over the text. Many others have contributed and have been acknowledged throughout the book.

Our research has been greatly helped by the excellent staff of the Cornish Studies Library, the Courtney Library and the Cornwall County Records Office; these are invaluable sources of information for local historians.

Proof reading is an onerous task – you get it right and no one notices but get it wrong and it's there for everyone to see. A special thanks, yet again, to our good friend Alan Murton from Goonhavern for carrying out this task.

The archive photographs appearing in this book are from many sources including Ken Young (photographer), the Clive Benney Collection and the Lambeth Palace Library. The present day photographs are by Tony Mansell.

References

Books:
A Book of the West – Revd S Baring-Gould
A History of Blackwater and its Neighbours – Clive Benney & Tony Mansell
A History of Cornwall – F E Halliday
Ancient and Holy Wells of Cornwall – The Misses Quiller-Couch
Cornwall - Gilbert
Cornwall, the Land of the Gods – Dr T F G Dexter
Friendly Retreat - Maruice Bizley
Jericho to Cligga - Clive Benney & Tony Mansell
Lake's Parochial History of Cornwall 1876.
Mithian in the parishes of St Agnes and Perranzabuloe – Tony Mansell
Old Cornish Crosses – A G Langdon
Portrait of a Village Church - Maurice & Alice Bizley
St Agnes and its Band – Tony Mansell
St Agnes 1001-1999 – Frank Carpenter
Sufferings of the Clergy – Dr Walker
The Book of St Agnes
The Cornish Handbook – John Kinsman
The St Agnes Guide Book of 1936
Tudor Cornwall – A L Rowse
West Britons – Mark Stoyle

Sundry articles and extracts from:
Journals of the St Agnes Museum Trust
Historical notes on the Parish by John King
St Agnes Parish Church Magazine
The Royal Cornwall Gazette
The Sherborne Mercury
The St Austell Gazette
The West Briton

Books by the same authors
Clive Benney:
      St Agnes Parish 1850-1920 A photographic record
      St Agnes Parish 1920-1950 A photographic record
      Around St Agnes - The Archive Photographic Series
      St Agnes - A Photographic History; Volume 1 - Down Quay
      St Agnes - A Photographic History; Volume 2 - Village & Shops
Tony Mansell:
      Mithian in the parishes of St Agnes and Perranzabuloe
      St Agnes and its Band
      Camborne Town Band
Clive Benney & Tony Mansell:
      A History of Blackwater and its Neighbours
      Jericho to Cligga